C000177399

AVIATION ARCHAEOLOGY

A collectors' guide to aeronautical relics

AVIATION ARCHAEOLOGY

A collectors' guide to aeronautical relics

Bruce Robertson

 Patrick Stephens, Cambridge

First edition – 1977
Second edition – 1983

ISBN 0-85059-638-6

Text set in 10 on 11 pt Helvetica Medium by
Foister & Jagg Ltd, Cambridge and
Blackfriars Press Ltd, Leicester.
Printed in England on 80 gsm Cream Antique
Wove Vol 18, and bound, by the Garden City
Press Ltd, Letchworth, for the publishers
Patrick Stephens Limited, Bar Hill,
Cambridge, CB3 8EL, England.

CONTENTS

INTRODUCING AERONAUTICA

Collecting is the mania of millions. If it is stamps, coins or antiques that you collect then there are a hundred guides readily available, giving you an idea of the various aspects of the subjects, scope, and relative values and sources of acquisition. Very little exists for aeronautical enthusiasts, hence this collector's guide.

It is only in recent years that the relics of our aeronautical heritage have become prized items. Within the lifetime of the majority of readers, including some teenagers, Spitfires were still being thrown on scrapheaps for metal salvage. The enthusiasts' journals of a dozen years ago were still recording wartime aircraft, including captured German and Japanese types, lying mouldering on scrapheaps around the country.

There came an awakening in the 1960s with an awareness of what had gone — not one example of a Stirling, Beaufort, Hampden or Whitley in existence, types which were built in four-figure quantities and were standard wartime operational aircraft. Of course some far-seeing enthusiasts had started preservation in the 1950s, but lack of funds to salvage what remained and lack of general interest led to much being lost. Now there is a consciousness of what is of value both by the Services and private individuals. We can take stock of what we have and what our future aims should be. The 1970s have become an age of relics and replicas for the privileged, and modelling aircraft past and present well within the pockets of all.

But it is not just complete aircraft that can attract collectors. The most prized components are propellers, items of armament and certain instruments. Many of those who dig at wreck sites are satisfied with a complete servo-motor unit, oleo leg or throttle control, and particularly a control column.

Apart from the pieces of actual aircraft, there is a vast range of material with aeronautical associations. The awards to airmen, aerial propaganda leaflets, the books and periodicals, tickets and cards, photos and paintings. The range is wide and open to all.

A neglected aspect of aeronautica is the exploration of the hundreds of disused airfields and the cataloguing of what remains and particularly a chronicling of their history. Many railway enthusiasts now spend their time re-tracing old closed lines, re-visiting the station buildings and noting the remains of bridges and crossings. There are also many disused airfields where runways, perimeter tracks and the sites of associated buildings can be traced out.

If any of these types of recreation, active or passive, appeal to you, read on.

VETERAN AND VINTAGE AIRCRAFT

Of all the items of aeronautica, what better than a complete aircraft? Efforts over the past few years have resulted in thousands of aircraft being preserved for posterity and it has become the ambition of many to have one of their own. But it is not just a matter of the initial acquisition of an aircraft; there are the problems of possible restoration, accommodation and maintenance. As a result the majority of enthusiasts associate themselves with organisations preserving the aircraft of the past.

Different organisations have different aims. There are those groups who believe it is essential that the aircraft function in their environment. But it is not a simple matter of restoring or maintaining in flying condition; such aircraft must be properly licensed and registered before they take to the air. The conditions and procedures are rigid and preparing and flying veteran and vintage aircraft is work for qualified engineers and pilots; this does not exclude enthusiasts playing an important part in the preparation under proper supervision.

Such are the skills involved in building replicas or restoring surviving aircraft, that some organisations have encouraged this work for their apprenticeship training. British Aviation, the Royal Air Force and the Royal Aircraft Establishment have all turned their apprentices to such work. Apart from the skills in metalwork and carpentry, there is the research into documentation to achieve accuracy, and in building or restoring a flying replica, there is the exacting thoroughness of the work, which is essential to safety. Moreover, there is a great sense of achievement, once the work has been completed and approved, with the first flight. Working in the past can be good training for the future.

Another school of thought is that genuine old aircraft types are too valuable to be risked in the air; no doubt they have in mind the surviving Bristol Bulldog presented by the Science Museum to the Shuttleworth Trust and destroyed in a crash on September 13 1964. On the other hand, flying veteran and vintage aircraft have, overall, a very good flight safety record; those who champion them point out that the greatest loss of veteran aircraft has occurred with static aircraft through hangar fires.

Preservation, restoration or replica

Whether flying or static, aircraft of historical importance come under three main categories; the preserved, the restored and the replica. The preserved are the genuine aircraft of the period. Typical examples are the World War 1 aircraft held by the Imperial War Museum. They were presented to the museum just after World War 1. They have had wings dismantled for moving and re-arrangement and have been repainted at times, but the original frames remain. As with most genuine World War 1 aircraft, the fabric deteriorates and needs replacing after the passage of time. This means that the outside surfaces and the paintwork are not original, but it is virtually impossible now to exhibit a World War 1 aircraft in its original state. So genuine old aircraft are inevitably restorations to some extent.

The restored aircraft are those found whole or in part in various stages of dilapidation and renovated by replacing rotting parts and manufacturing or substituting missing components. Then there is the replica, an aircraft made in modern times to the drawings of an old design. A typical example is the flying replica Vickers FB5 Gunbus built by the Vintage Aircraft and Flying Association (Brooklands) to celebrate the Royal Aeronautical Society's centenary in 1966. This aircraft is now on static display in the RAF Museum. Where no surviving example exists, a replica is a way of providing an example for exhibition. The majority of replicas are of World War 1 aircraft types and quite a number of private owners, particularly in America, own and fly replica Sopwith Pups, Camels and Triplanes and Fokker Triplanes; it has, in fact, become a facet of light plane sports flying.

To the replicas might be added the aircraft built for filming purposes but they are rarely truly representative, since modern light engines are fitted. Some of the aircraft for 'The Blue Max' were built in 12 weeks and while they served their purpose well, they are not to the standards of authenticity demanded by enthusiasts. There are, however, some exceptions.

Veteran and vintage guides

A leading question is how many veteran and vintage aircraft are there, of what types and where can they be seen? In Britain three museums in the London area have unrivalled collections in their own particular sphere, with many items of aeronautica in addition to complete veteran and vintage aircraft. Moreover admission is entirely free at the Science Museum, Kensington, the Imperial War Museum at Lambeth and the Royal Air Force Museum at Hendon.

As a guide to exhibitions, there are modestly priced booklets by Battle of Britain Prints International Ltd, 3 New Plaistow Road, London, E15 3JA (Telephone: 01-534-8833). Their three directories cover aircraft museums in Britain and Europe and vintage aircraft in the United Kingdom.

British Aircraft Preservation Council

There are many organisations interested in preserving aircraft of historical interest. Inevitably interests may clash and groups may be in competition with each other, on the other hand, where two similar examples are held by one group, an exchange could be of interest. The British Aircraft Preservation Society was formed in 1967 to co-ordinate all parties involved in such activities. Membership includes practically all major organisations interested in preservation, including national and private museums open regularly or periodically, or awaiting sites. Members are listed:

Aces High, Building D2, Fairoaks Airport, Chobham, Surrey.
Aeroplane Collection, 2 Bardell Crescent, Poynton, Cheshire.
Airborne Forces Museum, Browning Barracks, Aldershot, Hants.
Aircraft Preservation Society of Scotland, Currie, Midlothian.
Aircraft Radio Museum, Baginton, Coventry, Warks.

Air Historical Group, 8 Inglewood, St. John's, Woking, Surrey.

B-17 Ltd, 277 Chiswick High Road, London, W4 4PO.

Bristol Museum and Air Gallery, Queen's Road, Bristol, BS8 1RL.

Bristol Plane Preservation Unit, 'Green Winds', 10 Upper Town Lane, Bristol.

British Aerospace (Manchester Division) Anson Restoration Committee.

British Balloon Museum and Library (new member).

British Rotorcraft Museum, Delta House, Summer Lane, Warle, Weston.

Brooklands Museum of Aviation, Church Street, Weybridge, Surrey.

Chiltern Historical Aircraft Preservation Group, 16 Eskdale Avenue, Chesham, Bucks, HP5 3AX.

Cornwall Aircraft Park (Helston) Ltd.

Cotswold Aircraft Restoration Group, 82 Carrant Road, Mitton Estate, Tewkesbury, Gloucester GL20 8AD.

Dan-Air Preservation Group, 50 Queen Mary Avenue, Basingstoke.

Derby Industrial Museum, Silk Mill off Full Street, Derby DE1 3AR.

Derbyshire Historical Aviation Society, 263 Birchover Way, Allestree, Derby DE3 2RS.

Douglas Boston-Havoc Preservation Trust, 10 Adcote Close, Barwell, Leicestershire.

Dumfries & Galloway Aviation Group, 'Glensorrel', 68 Albert Road, Dumfries DG2 9DL. (Museum, Old Control Tower, Tinwald Downs.)

Durney Collection, 276 Weyhill Road, Andover, Hants.

Duxford Aviation Society, Duxford Airfield, Cambridgeshire.

East Anglian Aviation Society, 8 Pingle Lane, Northborough, Peterborough. (Museum at Control Tower, Bassingbourn Barracks, Herts.)

East Midlands Historic Flying Group (new member restoring a Varsity).

Essex Aviation Group, with display at Duxford Aerodrome.

Fenland Aircraft Preservation Society, 118 Edinburgh Drive, Wisbech.

Fleet Air Arm Museum, RNAS Yeovilton, Somerset BA22 8HT.

Historical Aircraft Museum, Aviation Way, Southend Airport, Essex.

Humberside Aircraft Preservation Society, with Museum at Cleethorpes.

Imperial War Museum, Lambeth Road, London, SE1 6HZ.

International Auster Pilot Club, 74 Manor Way, Deeping St. James, Peterborough PE6 8PX.

Kent Battle of Britain Museum, 35 Clifton Road, Welling, Kent.

Lashenden Air Warfare Museum, Headcorn Aerodrome, Kent.

Leicestershire Aircraft Preservation Group, 5 Oakland Avenue, Melton Road, Leicester LE4 7SG.

Leicestershire Museum of Technology, 96 New Walk, Leicester LE1 6TD.

Lincolnshire Aviation Museum, Old Railway Yard, Tattershall, Lincs.

Loughborough Leicestershire Air Museum and Preservation Society, 50 Tuckers Road, Loughborough, Leicestershire.

Manchester Museum of Air & Space, City Hall, Manchester.

Merseyside Aviation Society, 5 Barndale Road, Liverpool L18 1EN.

Midland Air Museum, Baginton, Coventry.

Military Aircraft Preservation Group, 51 Bleak Hey Road, Peel Hall, Wythenshawe, Manchester M22 5FS.

MM Aviation, Charlton Marshall, Blandford, Dorset.

Mosquito Aircraft Museum, Salisbury Hall, London Colney, Herts.

Moston College of Further Education, Ashley Lane, Manchester M9 1WU.

Museum of Army Flying, Middle Wallop, Stockbridge, Hants SO20 8DY.
Mustang International (aircraft based at Duxford).
Nene Valley Aviation Society, Sywell Aerodrome, Northants.
Newark Air Museum, Winthorpe Airfield, Newark.
Norfolk & Suffolk Aviation Museum. Exhibits at Flixton.
North East Aircraft Museum, Usworth.
Northern Aeroplane Workshops, 7 Scotton Drive, Knaresborough, Yorks.
North Weald Aircraft Restoration Flight (West Essex Wing ATC).
North Yorkshire Aircraft Recovery Centre (recently formed).
Norwich (City of) Aviation Museum, Norwich.
Pennine Aviation Museum, Moorfield Park, Bacup.
Personal Plane Services Ltd, Wycombe Air Park, Marlow, Bucks.
RAF Aerospace Museum, Cosford, Wolverhampton, West Midlands.
RAF Battle of Britain Memorial Flight, RAF Coningsby, Lincs.
RAF Museum, Aerodrome Road, Hendon, London NW9 5LL.
R. J. Mitchell Hall, Kingsbridge Lane, Southampton SO1 0GB.
Robertsbridge Aviation Society, 'Cwmavon', Northbridge Street, Robertsbridge, East Sussex (collection at Bush Barn).
Royal Aeronautical Society (Medway Branch) concerned with Spitfire Memorial Museum, RAF Manston, Kent.
Royal Scottish Museum of Flight, East Fortune.
Rural Flying Corps, Bourn Aerodrome, Cambridgeshire.
Russavia Collection, 'Peddars', Woodend Green, Henham, Bishops Stortford, Herts CM22 6AY.
Science Museum, Exhibition Road, South Kensington, London SW7.
Second World War Aircraft Preservation Society, 55 Melrose Walk, Basingstoke, Hants RG24 9HQ.
Scotland West Aircraft Investigation Group, 20 Braemar Crescent, Bearsden, Glasgow.
Scottish Aircraft Collection Trust (aircraft stored pending new museum).
Shuttleworth Collection, Aerodrome, Old Warden, Biggleswade, Beds.
Skyfame Aircraft Collection, Duxford Aerodrome, Cambridgeshire.
Solway Aviation Society, 132 Scotland Road, Carlisle, Cumbria.
South London Aircraft Recovery Group, 43 Eatonville Road, London SW17 7SH.
South Yorkshire Aviation Society, 31 Saffron Road, Tickhill, Yorks.
Strathallan Aircraft Collection, Auchterarder, Perthshire.
Surrey and Sussex Aviation Society, Atholl Cottage, Walpole Avenue, Chipstead, Surrey.
Torbay Aircraft Museum, Higher Blagdon, Near Paignton, Devon.
Ulster Folk and Transport Museum, Caltra Manor, Holywood, County Down, Northern Ireland.
Vintage Aircraft Club, 'Rosland', Main Street, West Hagbourne, Didcot, Oxon OX11 0NJ.
Vintage Aircraft Team, 72 Meadow Road, Bushey, Herts.
Vintage Glider Club of Great Britain (address as Russavia, housing at Duxford Aerodrome).
Viscount Preservation Trust, 17 Portsmouth Rd, Thames Ditton, Surrey.
Wales Aircraft Museum, 'Hafod-y-Bryn', 72 New Road, Llanelli.
Warbirds of Great Britain Ltd, Blackbushe Airport, Surrey.
Warplane Wreck Investigation Group, 34 Broughton Road, Wallesey.

Wartime Aircraft Recovery Group (Midlands area, display at Cosford).
Wealden Aviation Group, 77 Parkstone Road, Lower Ridge, Hastings.
Wessex Aviation Society, Knell Gardens, Wimborne, Dorset.
Winbolt Collection (radio, radar and navigation equipment).

In general, where a house name or number is given, the address is that of the nominated contact such as chairman or secretary. In addition to the list of council members named, there is an equally long list of associate members, including clubs, wreck investigation teams and magazines. The Council's Information Officer is Brian R. Robinson of 9 Brackley Road, Heaton Chapel, Stockport SK4 2QT.

American enterprise and the world at large

There are many preservation societies in America but no embracing national organisation, owing to the large numbers of owners and their diverse interests. With hundreds of licensed World War 1 replicas and surviving airworthy World War 2 aircraft, their outlook and scope are vastly different from those in Britain. America has a much larger population, far more space for flying and therefore less traffic congestion, as well as kinder weather.

An organisation, World War 1 Aeroplanes, was formed in 1961 in America to put builders and restorers of 1903-19 vintage aircraft in touch with each other, to help in finding engines, parts and drawings. An informative magazine is published five times a year edited by Leonard C. Opdyke, which nears its hundredth issue. For subscription details write to the organisation at 15 Crescent Road, Poughkeepsie, NY12601, USA.

One of the greatest achievements in the world of historic aircraft preservation is the Confederate Air Force of Texas which has around 100 aircraft, ranging from a Liberator to a Spitfire, making it the largest collection of flyable veteran aircraft in the world.

Worldwide efforts are being made to preserve and display the heritage of the air. Most European countries have national air museums and in Australia, Canada, South Africa and New Zealand preservation of old aircraft is taken as seriously as in Britain. The larger of the South American republics have air museums, and India has a national collection. But in Arab countries and the emergent African nations there is little interest, understandably as they have played little part in aeronautical development. However, in general, the countries of the world that have played their part in aeronautical development are as conscious of a need to preserve important historic aircraft as to maintain evidence of their architecture and culture.

Because of the upsurge of interest in preserving historic aircraft in recent years, most avenues have been explored leaving little chance of new finds of complete aircraft in out of way places. To obtain a more balanced presentation of aircraft types displayed will now largely depend on mutual co-operation, already well organised in Britain. But to provide examples of types not displayed, and to rectify component deficiencies in those that are, there is still a partly untapped source of supply — the ground. This means searching and digging out the remains of aircraft that crashed, an activity that has brought a new kind of aircraft enthusiast, the aviation archaeologist.

AVIATION ARCHAEOLOGY

A relatively new study, aviation archaeology expresses a desire, inherent in most of us, to explore. To progress to new ground in aeronautics means branching out into astronautics, which is the province of a privileged few sponsored on a national basis. But aviation archaeology offers an activity in which individuals can indulge and play a part in not only recalling the past, but revealing the past. As with true treasure seeking, there are disappointments, and it must be accepted that much of the tangled wreckage embedded in our soil is worthless both historically and commercially. But there is always the thought that you are on the verge of a great discovery.

Home ground

To discover crash sites, dig out the wreckage and restore parts is long, hard, painstaking work and there is little point in anyone entering this field of activity unless they are sustained by a fervent interest in aeronautics. If you have that, then the pursuit of aviation archaeology can grip you like prospectors in a gold rush. There has, in fact, been something of a rush over the past ten years and unfortunately wreck sites have been plundered rather than excavated in some cases.

There is always a hope that some rarer type of aircraft will be found well preserved in its entirety, but this is usually confined to marshy areas where salvage of anything, let alone a complete aircraft, can be difficult. You can tell whether or not examples of a particular aircraft type have been preserved by the reference books mentioned previously. You will find that no Stirlings, Hampdens, Whitleys or Beauforts are extant. On the other hand the number of Spitfires preserved runs into three figures, but this does not mean that values are lowered on this account. Spitfires are the most popular of all old aircraft and the type most enthusiasts hope to reconstruct, and they are always on the lookout for spares.

Observe the law

Before you set off to dig up a Spitfire, Messerschmitt 109 or any other aircraft type, you should be aware of one important factor — it's illegal! At least it is without official permission. Crashed British military aircraft are Crown property, as are also crashed German aircraft for they are deemed to be captured enemy material; the Ministry of Defence can exercise right of possession over aircraft of both categories. If it was a United States aircraft, operated by the USN, USAAF or USAF, the wreckage is the property of the United States Government for whom the British Ministry of Defence, by mutual agreement, act as representatives. In the case of a civil aircraft the ownership will rest with the owner or the insurers and may involve corres- pondence with the Air Registration Board and Lloyds.

The Ministry of Defence may give approval to recovery groups to investi- gate a United Kingdom crash site subject to their conditions set out in a leaflet. Permission, if granted, is limited to one year. For legal reasons per- ,mission has to be granted to named individuals on behalf of a group. Applica- tions and enquiries should be made Ministry of Defence (AFB Sec), Rm 8239 Main Building, Whitehall, London, SW1A 2HB. (Telephone: 01-218-3616 or 7136).

Permission by the Ministry of Defence implies no rights and certainly not exclusive right to recovery on a site; if more than one group want to work the same area the groups themselves must resolve who does the work and keeps the salvage. The Ministry on the other hand recognises the growing interest of enthusiasts in recovering, restoring and exhibiting aircraft, and their permission implies that they accept that those who recover parts may retain them in their possession.

However, a disquieting aspect of collecting items from digs became evident in 1974 when known enthusiasts were contacted by an organisation selling aircraft parts. A 50 × 20 cm area of sheet metal from a wing was offered at £4, rising to £25 for a length of Stirling propeller blade. These kind of activities are likely to endanger the granting of permission and bring the object of the investigations into disrepute.

There is still the question of permission to dig from the landowner to resolve — indeed, permission to enter his land. This is a matter for arrangements between the recovery group and the owner. Aircraft, par- ticularly fighters in a vertical dive, may go far into the ground, the engine ramming a hole and the wings breaking off. Such aircraft are embedded deep and it means much manual labour, perhaps drawn out over weeks, then a crane to finally lift the engine and a lorry for transit. Not many farmers are likely to welcome this sort of activity on their land, and usually their initial reaction is to refuse. If it is arable land, the farmer would hardly consider any digging while crops are growing — February to September. Farmers by and large are not aircraft enthusiasts and may never have heard of aircraft recovery groups. To an approach from a group prepared to actively dig in his soil, his reaction is often similar to that of an approach made by an oil drilling company — what will be his share of the mineral rights? Do you honestly expect him to believe that a team of people, set to dig up his land, are doing so without thought of financial reward? He needs some convincing in Britain in the 1980s.

The approach is all important. There is a great temptation to reconnoitre a site first before the tedium of getting permission, but if you are found trespassing by the owner you are at an immediate disadvantage in obtain- ing permission to dig. To attempt an exploratory dig without permission could bring legal penalties. The best approach is to tell the landowner that you are aircraft enthusiasts and that you have reasons to believe, which can be expounded, that a certain aircraft crashed on his land. The showing of your membership cards of an enthusiasts' organisation might help. Then come round to the question of exploring the site and arrange as necessary further meeting in case you want to go all out to dig. At all times be courteous and close gates securely behind you. If it does come to full permission to dig, you must expect the farmer to ask some guarantee that his land will be left as it was found. In the interests of the reputation of every recovery group you must remember that your dig does not finish when you've dug out all there is to find, but when the land has been restored to normal.

Many crashes have occurred because aircraft flew into high ground and wreckage is strewn about on the surface on remote and rocky areas. In such cases the land administration such as the Snowdonia National Park Authority or National Trust, as appropriate, should be contacted before any parts are removed. There is usually no objection to the removal of unsightly wreckage blighting the landscape. On the other hand, through a growing interest in aeronautica, the wreckages have become points of interest on mountain walks and provide landmarks. So, because wreckage is lying on the surface in rocky areas, it does not mean that it can be removed without the consent of the authority for the land.

During the war maps were prepared to show the number of crashes that occurred on high ground to chart the Royal Observer Corps posts placed best to fire rocket warnings to aircraft heading for high ground. These charts, issued under the code name 'Granite', should be found in the Public Record Office.

Crash circumstances

Crash site investigations fall into two main categories. Those where a wreckage site is evident from local gossip or has been found without linkage to the event, and those sites found because it is known that a particular aircraft crashed in the vicinity and that the site found is most probably the actual spot where it went in. There are significant differences between the two categories. In the first case it is not known what to expect, not even the type of aircraft; some searchers prefer the element of surprise and the deductions which result. In the second case, a site from documentation on a crash report, the aircraft type, mission and the fate of crew are likely to be known. It may be asked that, if information is known for some crashes, why not for all? This disparity occurs because records exist by aircraft type and serial number; the fate of each aircraft can be traced, but there is no comparable cross-reference whereby you look up a parish and find out what aircraft crashed in the vicinity. Such cross-referencing would not be a simple matter since crash records cover every type of accident, including mere heavy landings on airfields, making a prodigious clerical task, involving tens of thousands of reports.

In either case there is a further record that could be sought and that is the salvage reports of the time, which should be in the Public Record Office, but may be difficult to track down. Some recovery groups insist on the fullest documentation before tackling any site and avoid those where there are likely to be embarrassing items.

Sensibilities

While crew may have baled out from wrecks or their bodies removed by the RAF just after the crash, the fact is that there is a likelihood of coming across human remains. In such a case the remains should not be touched and should be treated with due respect. The police and the Ministry of

Defence should be informed and all activity on the site suspended until the remains have been removed. A coroner's court may be involved and the recovery team required to give evidence. If it is a documented dig, the pilot's identity may be known, but on no account should this information be made known to other than the police until the Ministry of Defence have contacted any known next of kin or relatives. One has only to read the 'In Memoriam' columns of some of our daily newspapers to realise that the loss of beloved husbands, brothers, sons and fathers is still most deeply felt, and distress could be caused to relatives unless groups conduct themselves with the utmost decorum.

Items found such as cigarette cases, are likely to be private property and should be handed in to the police with a brief note of their discovery. It is also a condition of Ministry of Defence permission that the discovery of any books, papers, maps, etc, will be notified to the Ministry who will decide if the recovery group can retain such documents.

Dangers

The element of danger in recovery should be fully realised and a small first aid kit is a wise precaution. Jagged edges are likely to result from a violent impact with the ground and cuts frequently occur in the unravelling. Any such wounds should be treated with antiseptic. For small cuts plastic bandages should be applied to avoid the cut being open to further infection.

When digging deep, dig wide although this calls for increased labour; it will prevent caving in which could have fatal results. Some items may be weighty and could crush if not handled properly. If it has not already become apparent, it should be realised now that recovery is for group work not for individuals. A length of rope is always useful and particularly as a safety measure. If any item is likely to topple if moved, it may be possible to loop the rope around the part and shift it from a safe distance. Heavy sections moved up from the digging area should always be tugged up by ropes, never pushed up. Apart from the outside skin, as veteran diggers will know, aircraft structures have spaces in ribs and plates to reduce aircraft weight through which rope can be securely tied. The responsibility for any injury sustained is not in question — it's your own. There are even graver dangers.

Ammunition and explosives

The fact has to be faced that fighter and bomber aircraft were weapons systems. The whole point of their production was to bring guns to bear and carry bombs to drop. Ammunition, including cannon shells, bombs both incendiary and high explosive, pyrotechnics such as signal flares, and equipment detonators, may well be found in wreckage.

Ammunition has had a fascination for many — it could be a fatal fascination. Rounds of ammunition were prized souvenirs of both world wars. The areas around crashed German airships in World War 1 swarmed with souvenir hunters and to a lesser degree around some crashed German aircraft in World War 2, particularly in the early years. In spite of the removal of parts being against the Defence Regulations then in force, many rounds found their way home to cupboards and many were displayed on mantelpieces — immediately above an open hearth!

Over the years the public have become far better educated on the dangers from explosives and all should be aware that the unauthorised holding of arms or ammunition is an offence under the Firearms Act 1968 and the Explosives Act 1875. When firearms or explosives are found the police should be notified and work suspended until the site is declared safe. Rounds of .303 ammunition are frequently found scattered over a wide area and should be carefully collected and handed to the police for disposal.

There is always the danger that explosives will not be recognised as such. Before the war all service bombs were yellow and practice bombs black with yellow bands, but to avoid compromising camouflage of airfields they were finished in dull green from the late 1930s (excepting practice bombs, which were white) with bands of different colour to indicate different fillings. The code has not been included here since all material found suspected as being of an explosive nature should be dealt with by the proper authorities who will be notified through the police.

Ammunition and bomb cases are, of course, items displayed and kept as souvenirs. In the RAF a move was made as early as 1928 to vet all such souvenirs, following the accidental explosion of a bomb used for decoration purposes in an officers' mess. After that, all similar acquisitions had to be inspected by an armament officer and then marked either as 'EMPTY' or 'DUMMY WEIGHTED'.

A new trend is developing that might lead to complications — that of replica ammunition. Lemarka Reproductions recently offered 'something completely new and exciting for modellers and military enthusiasts — the first time ever'. This was a full size, 34-inch long replica (not model) of a German 88 mm armour-piercing shell as used in anti-aircraft guns, described as completely authentic in finish. Harmless enough, but the very fact such an item is marketed does show the fascination that there is for ammunition. Do not be tempted to collect the real thing when you can get a very realistic and safe substitute. There is, too, a possible danger from fire or an explosion by petrol. In general this will have seeped out and evaporated, but as diggers will know, a crash spot often reeks of fuel and it is possible that pockets of petrol have been trapped; therefore no smoking is an advisable precaution.

The point has already been made that recovery is for group work and not for individuals. From the foregoing it should also be evident that it is not a job for a happy-go-lucky crowd armed with picks and shovels setting out for a suspected wreck site, but a job that has to be carefully pre-planned. To participate in such activities it is advisable to become a member of an organisation.

Aviation Archaeologists' Association

The Aviation Archaeologists' Association (AAA) was founded in 1973 to encourage and assist the efforts of those engaged in the research and recovery of aircraft wrecks of World War 2, unite those with common interests and record their activities. It was thought that the pooling of knowledge could only be of benefit to those concerned and reduce the possibility of duplicated research. The association supports various museums and hopes to establish a museum of its own. Most important of all, the association urges that all activities be conducted with due observance of the necessary formalities.

Membership of the association costs a modest sum annually and entitles members to a restricted circulation magazine giving accounts of regional activities, wreck logs of certain aircraft types, occasional articles on identification of components, and crash site reports.

The association's so-called 'AAA Sortie Reports' set out in the following form, are something of a model for crash site reporting:

Aircraft type, Mark, serial number, coding, unit, base.

Crash location, giving hill or farm name, parish and county.

Ordnance Survey map reference. Height above sea level if relevant and date of crash.

Access from nearest road with directions.

Site details giving a description of the site as found and what was yielded.

History of the aircraft's last flight giving nature of sortie and fate of crew.

Notes relevant to the site such as landowner.

Your crash site recording

While the AAA's Sortie Reports have considerable merit in setting out details, a slightly different form is recommended as follows:

Aircraft type, Mark and serial number.

Unit, coding, base.

Date of crash and location with pinpoint reference, including note on area.

Background of crash, nature of sortie, fate of crew, etc.

Salvage report at the time.

Ministry of Defence permission reference.

Access details and landowner.

Site details and work done.

The reason for this arrangement is to have in mind at the outset whether or not explosives are likely to be encountered, to place together all details of the aircraft at the time and follow through with the subsequent events in chronological sequence. And, most important of all, to end with the site work which will be a most extensive entry as each find is logged and its disposal recorded. It is appreciated that a salvage report at the time may not be traced. Indeed, it may be a crash site found where even the aircraft type is not known. Nevertheless, the heading should be included and space left for your digging may provide the answers.

Official crash records

There are no such things as official crash records; there are, however, accident records under various categories such as Flying, Ground, MT, etc. Certain briefs on accidents from around the mid-1930s are held by the Air Historical Branch of the Ministry of Defence, but being originally Flight Safety statistical record cards they were designed for quick reference to the types of accident, eg birdstrikes, undercarriage failures, tyrebursts, etc, and are not suitable for a quick check on a site. A so-called Stats Card also exists on each aircraft filed by type and serial number, which will give a unit and normally the date of accidents and final write-off, but apart from giving a crash category (see page 72) they give no indication of crash location.

From the 1920s it has been decreed by the Air Council that all RAF units at home and abroad where flying is carried out will keep a complete record of all flying accidents and forced landings on Form 764. During World War 2 flying accidents, forced landings and engine failures were reported on Form 765C titled *Report on Flying Accident or Forced Landing not attributable to Enemy Action* (Forms 765A and B were concerned with unit establishment of aircraft and flying hours). The object of Form 765C was to provide a unit record of the accident, give headquarters and authorities concerned an early short report of the accident, and to set out what happened, and why it happened, in a form that could be used for compiling statistics such as the accident cards mentioned.

Form 765 was revised in December 1941 and February 1943 so that the format varied slightly throughout the war.

Aircraft crashing due to enemy action were not documented to the same degree. They did not need to be at the time since they did not provide valuable flight safety statistics. Brief details may occur on the Form 541 (see page 58) for each unit held in the Public Record Office.

Crash areas

With aviation archaeology there is the constant linkage with records. The finding of a crash site and the search for the story behind it; or coming across notice of the crash in records and finding the precise spot. By far the most crashes occur on landing or take-off and so it is in the vicinity of airfields that the majority of crash sites exist. The airfields of World War 1 are tabulated in Appendix A, and the World War 2 airfields are mapped out elsewhere in this book.

It would take several books to detail all the crashes that occurred in Britain alone during the last war, but to give some idea of the vast extent of the subject, the major accidents occurring in just one unit, at one airfield, in one year of the war — No 14 Operational Training Unit at Cottesmore, near Oakham, Rutland (as it was then), during 1942 — are tabled:

January 26	Hampden I P1186 dived in ½ mile north of North Pinchbeck railway station.
February 15	Hampden I L6020 abandoned in air. Fell at Risegate.
February 16	Hampden I AE386 crashed on take-off at Saltby satellite
March 8	Hampden I L4110 crashed on landing circuit, two miles NW Saltby satellite.
March 13	Hampden I AD988 dived in at Thistleton (three miles north of airfield).
March 25	Hampden I P1298 hit lorry on airfield when landing.
March 25	Hampden I P5398 crashed at Whittle Farm, Brock Hampton.
March 27	Hampden I L4108 crashed on airfield doing practice night landing.
April 19	Oxford I AS902 crashed at night at Cold Overton, ten miles from base.
May 2	Hampden I P1277 hit Saltby boundary and burst into flames.

May 5	Hampden I AE186 swung on take-off and took fire.
May 5	Hampden I P1351 yawed after take-off from Saltby and crashed at Stonesby.
May 15	Oxford I AT479 destroyed in collision with Hampden while landing.
May 31	Hampden I P5321 destroyed in mid-air collision over Plantation Farm, Whitmore.
June 3	Oxford I AS904 wrecked ½ mile east of Greetham village.
June 6	Hampden I L4133 spun in at Mere Barn, South Stoke (two miles east of Saltby).
June 16	Hampden I AD787 swung landing at Saltby and burnt out.
June 30	Hampden I AD802 crashed at Gunthorpe Bridge attempting to land at Saltby.
June 30	Hampden I AD848 dived in at Moorends near Doncaster.
July 12	Hampden I X2974 crashed at East Stoke after collision with Wellington.
July 30	Hampden I P5397 fell at Windsor Farm, Langtoft, after colliding with Hampden AE192.
August 1	Hampden I P2129 crashed a mile SW of airfield.
August 18	Hampden I AE155 apparently dived in, near Edenham village.
August 13	Anson I R9608 hit boundary.
August 28	Hampden I AE312 dived vertically into Thistleton village (two miles from airfield).
August 31	Hampden I P1205 struck ground on low run, Grimthorpe Bombing Range.
September 2	Hampden I L4162 dived vertically on approach near Thistleton (three miles NE of airfield).
September 15	Hampden AD740 dived in landing at airfield.
September 30	Wellington 1C T2747 flew into ground in low cloud at Market Overton.
October 1	Wellington IC R1401 stalled on airfield.
November 8	Hampden I L4100 undershot Saltby crashing a mile east.
November 9	Wellington IC X3163 overshot airfield, crashed at Barrow a mile SW.
December 2	Wellington IC L7850 forced landed at Eaton Park, three miles SE of airfield.
December 4	Wellington IC DV929 crashed Cottesmore village after night take-off.
December 6	Wellington IC R1522 crashed near Barrow village after night take-off (one mile W of airfield).
December 17	Wellington IC R1603 crashed on edge of Harlaxton airfield.
December 21	Wellington IC T2887 forced landed Millhill Farm, near Bingham, after engine fell out.

It will be seen that the majority of the accidents occurred on the aerodrome or its satellite field at Saltby. It is around such areas that land can be searched speculatively. Local gossip may well lead to a precise location and the village inn is a good place to start. You may get some good leads, particularly if you stand a round. But be warned that memories are notoriously unreliable, and time tends to become telescoped. A verbal report may be true and still lead to a fruitless search. One group were given a vivid account by local people, at Anstey, some five miles north-west of Leicester, of an aircraft crashing at High Lea Farm. This proved true enough. It was early in the war and so had a greater impact on the local population, many of who went to view the wreck lying in a field. Hampden P1310, so it transpired, was overtaken by thickening fog and the pilot took the first opportunity to make a wheels-up landing in a field. On its belly it looked much like a wreck, but in fact the complete aircraft was salvaged. Not one piece remained.

On arable or pasture land you can expect the farmer to have removed any pieces of metal from the surface, even supposing the salvage team at the time left pieces about. Recently ploughed land sometimes reveals pieces, for it is a fact that material may well be thrown up by one particular ploughing that has hitherto been buried below the surface for years. This has been the experience of many farmers of the World War 1 battlefields in Belgium and France.

Another sign, and an ominous one, is a purplish tinge to the earth. This usually indicates the site of a wreck that burnt out. Usually there is little to be found, fabric will have been burnt up, magnesium alloys may have powdered and other metal parts greatly distorted by heat. In summer such sites can usually be located by the stunted growth of grass or crops.

Metal detectors

A metal detector is one of the prime aids in finding crash sites, not only speculatively for even when a location by map reference is known, it is often difficult to assess a particular spot and the detector comes into its own. There are many different models on the market at various prices and several are advertised regularly in the Exchange and Mart.

The newcomer to wreck searching needs to consider several factors when selecting his instrument. Sensitivity is the major factor — the area it will sweep and the depth to which it will probe. This will vary according to the strength which is usually proportional with the price. A good detector will react to a large object up to ten feet beneath the surface of the earth, but small objects would only be detected at inches.

Indications can be in three main forms: earphones, speaker or meter. In the first two there will be an audible tuning note when metal is detected and in the last-named a pointer will visibly jump. Battery type, endurance and weight are other considerations; one make specifies 300 hours life from a PP3 battery, while another offers only 40 hours, but this may well be proportional to sensitivity. The more powerful the detector, the heavier it will be on batteries.

Weight can be an important consideration for those spending a whole day on a detection trek. It is not just the carrying that is wearying, but arm fatigue in holding the instrument in the working position. The majority of detectors currently marketed weigh from one to five pounds. A wide range of detectors is available from just under £40 up to £600, and some models can be adapted for use in water. In general the cheaper detectors react only to ferrous metals so that their use is limited in view of the duralumin of

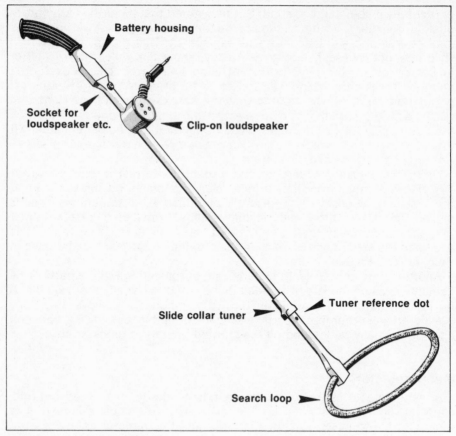

Typical simple metal detector.

which most aircraft structures were made having only 15 per cent iron, but inevitably certain components, and the mass of the engine, were largely of ferrous metals. Special detectors are available to react to non-ferrous metals, at a price.

Aviation archaeologists form but a small proportion of those searching the ground, the vast majority being the coin and treasure seekers. There are only some 500 professional archaeologists in the true sense of the word, and about the same number of active aviation archaeologists, although thousands of others are interested in the subject — but over 100,000 metal detectors have been sold and they are still selling. Every new find of a hoard of treasure reported in the press, brings a new spate of treasure hunters whose activities in many of our beauty spots are becoming as much of a nuisance as transistor radios. These treasure seekers are much disliked by the professionals, for with lack of knowledge they often destroy much of value. There have been confrontations between the amateurs and the professionals and between treasure seekers and park wardens. The aviation archaeologist should therefore be aware that, armed with a detector, he is most likely to be thought to be another of the treasure hunters and should note that on some public land, regulations have been amended to forbid detectors.

Detector licensing and consultants

Until 1981, detectors for non-ferrous metals required a licence from the Home Office for a 'Pipe Finder', but this is no longer required. Certain large commercial detecting appliances may require licensing under the Wireless Telegraphy Acts, but the normal apparatus used by enthusiasts does not come into this sphere.

Before buying any apparatus from an electronics dealer it is best to look around and get the brochures on the various makes and judge their suitability for your purpose. General electrical goods suppliers do not always stock metal detectors and they do not constitute a subject heading in the Post Office's Yellow Pages supplements. Some firms specialise in metal detectors. In the south-east there is Joan Allen Electronics Limited who are metal detector retailers and consultants, situated at 184 Main Road, Biggin Hill, Kent (Telephone: 0959-71255/6/7). When getting advice, make a point of stressing your particular requirement, as the majority of detector buyers are 'treasure' (as opposed to wreckage) hunters. Hire purchase terms are available for buyers and some firms offer special discounts for cash payment. With some makes there are service and warranty assurances lasting for several years, so it is as well to study the literature available.

Coastal areas

The sea bed holds many a wreck but salvage in deep waters would be an involved and expensive business. Closer inshore there are a number of wrecks, such as on the Goodwin sands where Lancasters and Fortresses can be seen at times of exceptionally low tide. Some sub-aqua clubs have co-operated with aviation archaeologists, and local trawling has brought up aircraft parts.

There are, however, grave dangers attendant with the examination of submerged wrecks. This was tragically demonstrated on October 16 1975. A trawler's net fouled a wreck off Newhaven and a diver from Eastbourne was called to free the net. He did not surface and it can only be presumed that he was caught up in the wreckage.

Another difficulty with offshore wrecks is that they cannot be accurately pinpointed. To give specific examples, known offshore ditchings in January 1942 amounted to nine but their official locations are as nebulous as follows: Anson from AOS, Penrhos, six miles west of Llanbedr; Wellington from No 15 OTU, two miles from Portreath; Anson attached to PRU, St Eval, near Fishpool, Newquay; Albacore of 774 Squadron, St Merryn, off Portqueen Bay; Swordfish from RNAS St Merryn, two miles off Boscastle; Wellington from Mildenhall, just off Spurn Point; Wellington of No 407 Squadron, two miles off Hornsea; Hampden of No 106 Squadron, three miles off Cromer; Halifax of No 76 Squadron, three miles from Greyness.

This is just a month's coastal losses at a time when operations were at a fairly low profile compared with the war years to follow. In each case the aircraft is believed unsalvaged. The Halifax floated for an hour and an attempt was made to tow it in, but at 10.34 hours on January 30 it went down in deep water where it still remains. Aircraft crashing close inshore could be pinpointed much more accurately and a Wellington in February 1942 went in only an estimated 300 yards from a Martello Tower (precise tower withheld in case some amateur swimmers take risks). Incidentally, if sea salvage is attempted, as well as Ministry of Defence permission, the local Receiver of Wreck must establish ownership.

Wreck site guide books

Several enthusiasts' organisations have produced books that give a guide to wreck sites. First published in 1961, the very latest edition of the Merseyside Aviation Society's *Wrecks and Relics* is available from the Society or from any of the specialist aviation bookshops. This detailed book lists, by counties, the preserved, derelict, wrecked and instructional aircraft in the UK. *White Rose Base*, by Brian Rapier, deals with World War 1 and 2 air activities over Yorkshire, including crash sites, and S. Finn in *Lincolnshire Air War 1939-1945* lists hundreds of crash sites in that county; both books are well illustrated. The Warplane Wreck Investigation Group have published a Halifax crash log and similar booklets are currently being compiled. With soft covers, and produced by enthusiasts, all these booklets are modestly priced and can be obtained from the larger bookshops that specialise in aircraft publications; they are also advertised from time to time in the aeronautical monthlies.

Wrecks around Europe

The RAF lost 57,000 aircraft during World War 2 and a large number of these fell in Western Europe. The high density loss areas were Northern France, Belgium, Holland and Denmark. Many of these aircraft lie embedded in the ground and in lakes and rivers. The Luftwaffe kept record of every Allied aircraft crash known to them on a special form and over 8,000 had been compiled by the spring of 1944. Each form was given a serial number of the German salvage organisation and details were filed under headings — Location, Date, Type, Unit, Base, Markings, etc, ending with spaces for details on special installations. The forms were submitted to Intelligence who in some cases took photographs as well as investigating before disposal was authorised. Salvage was then carried out thoroughly with a view to recovering the maximum of metal. In the Occupied territories, the local people were usually first on the scene and many aircraft parts were carried away and buried to prevent them falling into German hands.

However, when it comes to general relics of the two world wars, it is a fact that far more relics of World War 1 are found than of World War 2 in France and Belgium.

France and Belgium — World War 1

During the 1914-18 war a total of 55,093 airframes were built in Britain and a further 3,051 were purchased from France and America for the British flying services. By the end of 1918, 25,000 aircraft were still on order and to keep unemployment down 13,432 were delivered in 1919. France during that war built 67,982 aircraft, Italy some 20,000 and America 15,000, while Germany and Austria built 47,637. Yet the survival rate of genuine 1914-18-built aircraft is exceedingly low — whatever happened to them all?

Airframes of the period were of wood and fabric, both combustible materials, but engines were of metal and engine production roughly matched airframe production. It is aircraft engines of the period that are more likely to be found than airframes. A compact mass of metal, weighing several hundred pounds, hurtling to earth, makes a deep hole and the engines of many aircraft shot down in the 1914-18 war still lie in the soil of France and Belgium. Many were, of course, salvaged at the time, but two main areas could not then be reached and have been largely forgotten since.

The first, and obvious area, is in the vicinity of 'No Man's Land', the territory between the trenches of the opposing forces. Strictly, 'No Man's Land' was the area between the front line trenches stretching from the Belgian coast to the Swiss frontier. The width varied from 100 yards to a mile according to the part of the front, but in effect the non-salvageable area was a mile or so forward of each front — the area that could be swept by machine-gun or rifle fire. Any aircraft coming down in these areas would be destroyed by the opposing side's field guns, but only a direct hit would destroy an engine and many were buried as a result of such fire. The line varied from time to time, particularly after the larger battles, like the Somme, Arras, etc, and the British Front varied from 80 miles in mid-1917 to 100 in March 1918 and 60 in November 1918. Taking into account the length, variations, and the two-mile width where salvage would have been difficult, several hundred square miles of territory are involved.

The second large area concerns rivers, the French Aisne, Ancre, Escault, Lys, Oise, Sambre, Scarpe, Schelde and Somme, including the areas they flooded in winter, and in particular the Yser. The Yser, rising in France, enters Belgium after flowing 23 miles and empties into the North Sea after a further 26 miles. At the French frontier it is only some 12 yards wide but it widens to some 50 yards at the estuary. When the Germans attacked through Belgium in 1914, their advance was stayed by the desperate measure of flooding the area by breaching the banks with gunfire and by destroying the sluices at Nieuport which normally held back the incoming sea, and at ebb-tide permitted the discharge of the river. A vast area was flooded over which many aerial battles took place and into which aircraft fell and disappeared in the mud and have remained there after the post-war land reclamation. Incidentally, during the Battle of the Yser, monitors bombarded the Germans, aided by observation from the air, making it the first battle waged on land, sea and air.

Apart from the Yser flooding, the whole of the low-lying Ypres area, with its canals and Yser tributaries, were flooded from time to time, and many aircraft fell here which have never been recovered. But there are many snags in searching the area. Firstly, French and Belgian views on metal detectors, and the false readings that would come from the millions of shells that ended up in the mud and are still being unearthed. There is also little local interest in uncovering what might remain of aircraft engines, in areas where houses still bear scars resulting from that war.

Dunkirk is particularly significant for bearing the scars of aerial warfare. The French port of Dunkirk had both a French Navy and Royal Naval Air Service seaplane station, aerodrome and depot in World War 1, and the town was raided 177 times by German aeroplanes apart from Zeppelin raids: it was also under artillery bombardment. Many of these scars, regarded by most tourists as evidence of the fateful days of 1940, were actually sustained in the earlier world war.

One particular site for investigation is Boisdinghem. Adjacent the air-field a great circular pit was dug to take the surplus aircraft after the Armistice. Captain R. Sykes has given his impressions when he arrived there in Sopwith Camel F5941 on January 23, 1919. Mechanics removed the clock and Aldis gunsight from the aircraft, cut through the bracing with bolt cutters to collapse the wings and reduce the space the aircraft would take up, and wheeled and tipped it into the pit which, when full, was filled over with earth. What a site for investigation — and similar disposal spots.

Western Europe — World War 2

On the Continent in France, Belgium, Holland and Germany, and parts of Britain, the most prolific of the vestiges of aerial warfare is 'Window'. It still litters thousands of square miles in Western Europe, now tainted brown and looking like part of the earth and rarely recognised for what it is. 'Window' was the code name for the strips of tin foil dropped to cause responses on enemy radar and swamp the instruments with blips so that aircraft could not be picked out. It was used against both approach-detecting and gun-ranging radars, and was dispensed from RAF aircraft from the night of July 24/25 1943 until the end of war. The Germans retaliated over Britain, dropping similar foil from October 7 1943.

The foil was in strips 25 cm long and 2 cm wide, packaged in 2 lb bundles containing about 2,200 strips each, which were dispensed at the rate of a bundle per minute from each aircraft. After dropping it took 20 to 30 seconds to disperse and then 15 - 20 minutes to reach the ground, drifting in the wind, so that it fell over a wide area.

Antwerp has special significance in aerial warfare, as the area to sustain the heaviest missile bombardment, being the target for both V1 pilotless aircraft and V2 rocket bombardment. The V1s normally exploded on con-tact, but the V2s went deep and exploded leaving large craters strewn with mutilated pieces of A4 rocket which were filled in by British Army pioneer teams in the city and by farmers in the locality. From the air the crater marks can still be discerned in winter by the slight change in colour, due chiefly to chalk thrown up.

The Low Countries

It is estimated that some 6,800 aircraft of the RAF, USAAF and Luftwaffe crashed in the Netherlands during World War 2. The majority of wrecks were dealt with by German salvage teams at the time, but some 1,000 are believed to have fallen in coastal areas and inland waters. For over 50 years the Dutch have been concerned with the vast 820 square mile land reclamation scheme in the Zuider Zee. In the 1960s some of the polders were isolated and drained, revealing many wrecked American, British and German aircraft, some almost complete. Since the object of the scheme was to cultivate the area, the wrecks represented a hazard to agricultural machinery and the Luchtmacht Bergingsdienst (Aircraft Evacuation Ser-vice) of the Royal Netherlands Air Force were tasked with the clearance of the wrecks with all that it involved in the disposal of bodies and explo-sives. Among the wrecks revealed were a complete Fortress and Lancaster, the remains of a Gotha IV shot down in World War 1, and a Mosquito with German ammunition suggesting that it was of the German KG200 'Spy Squadron'.

The Departmental Chief of the Public Information Service of the Royal Netherlands Air Force, Major A. P. de Jong, has done much to keep all interested informed and Gerrit Zwanenburg of the Dutch Ministry of Defence has been involved in much of the wreck identification work. As a result most wrecks in the Netherlands are now dealt with by experts.

There were also a considerable number of aircraft wrecks in Belgium, but the great majority were fairly accessible to the German salvage teams. Relatively few wrecks of World War 2 lie undiscovered in the territory, one of the most heavily populated countries in the world, but quite possibly there are some wrecks of World War 1 beneath the soil. Surprisingly, the Allied disarmament teams in 1945 found few German aircraft in the Low Countries, their official figures being nil for Holland, and three Ju 88s plus one each FW 200, Ju 52, Do 217, Bf 109 and Bf 110 for Belgium. These official figures give a false impression, as the aircraft collected before hostilities ceased by RAF salvage teams are not included in the official disarmament totals.

Scandinavia

The magnificent efforts in recent years of salvaging a Halifax and Gladiator from Norwegian fjords for British museums have received much publicity, but such exploits are the results of expeditions. In general Norway and Sweden have only isolated crash sites, in contrast to Denmark where there is almost a concentration. The crash sites throughout Denmark have come under the close scrutiny of a dedicated researcher — Jorge Helme. A private pilot with an interest in aeronautical history, his quest started while on holiday in Svino, Southern Jutland, when coming upon the graves of 60 Commonwealth airmen. Since then he has tracked down, as far as possible, the crash sites of over 250 Allied aircraft and ascertained the fate of the occupants.

A number of pictures of the crash sites at the time are held by the Danish Resistance Museum in Copenhagen. While most of the wrecks were dealt with by German salvage teams at the time, it often took time to get to the various islands that comprise Denmark and many parts were buried or hidden by the Danes to prevent them falling into German hands; these occasionally come to light. There are several complete wrecks in water, off parts of Denmark, one reported as Mustang III ex-No 19 Squadron in 15 feet of water 200 yards offshore. Several other offshore wrecks are known to fishermen who at times catch their nets in them.

At the end of hostilities British Disarmament Wings recorded 1,146 German aircraft in Denmark and 579 in Norway which they destroyed and handed over to these two countries as scrap metal. Among them were the remains of 381 Bf 109s and 344 FW 190s.

Western Desert and Mediterranean islands

The dramatic story of the finding of a Liberator in the North African desert with coffee still drinkable in a vacuum flask has given rise to an impression that the Western Desert might yield much more. Unfortunately that time has passed. The campaign in the Western Desert was followed quickly by the invasion of Sicily and Italy and the wreckage was left strewn over the Western Desert. Among these abandoned aircraft wrecks visible from the coastal road from Egypt just after the war were Spitfire IXs MH530 TJ:J and MJ512, Catalina JX327, Stirling Vs PJ890 and PJ953, Dakota KN251, Beaufighter EL504, Baltimore IIIAs FA149 and FA270, and Fiat G50 MM6028. It was thought that they would remain indefinitely — but their turn came. The local Arabs soon became aware of the value of scrap metal and after dealing with the more lucrative items such as guns and fighting vehicles, eventually disposed of the aircraft as well.

The most rewarding areas for searching out wrecks are small islands over which there has been intensive aerial activity. Malta will spring to many minds, but it is one of the most densely populated areas of the world and there are few stones on its soil that have been left unturned; moreover, it is not a soil to absorb as it is a topsoil on rock. It is the sea around Malta that has much yet to reveal in German, Italian and British aircraft; but since there is also much of general archaeological value the Maltese Government have stringent rules for sub-aqua and similar club activities.

More rewarding are the more sparsely populated islands Crete and Sicily, where World War 2 wrecks were abandoned because they were not worth salvage involving sea transportation. On Crete there are the German glider wrecks adapted by the locals as shelters as well as wrecks strewn around the island.

Sicily is perhaps the island most likely to reward searchers. There were over a thousand wrecked aircraft at ten airfields on the island at one point in the war. Pantelleria too, the island between Sicily and Cape Bon on the North African coast, was practically abandoned after 1943, with numbers of aircraft strewn around. While only five aircraft were left in the bricked underground hangars hewn out of a hillside — a Bf 109 under repair, a Macchi 205 and Reggiane 2001, and two Ca 164 training biplanes, spread around the airfield were six Bf 109s, 14 Fiat G-50s, ten Macchi 202s, nine Fiat Cr 42s, six Fiat Cr 25s, three Reggiane 2001s, seven Macchi 200s, seven SM 79s, five SM 81s, nine SM 82s and single examples of Ju 52, Fi 156 Storch and Macchi 205, plus some 60 aero engines. They were abandoned by the Germans and Italians, and soon by-passed by the Allies as they moved on to Sicily and Italy. The Allies had no use for the aircraft for spares and their metal salvage value was not worth the efforts of a Repair and Salvage Unit transporting and shipping for smelting. In any case, the harbour and town had been reduced to a shambles. So what happened to these aircraft? Here is a site for investigation.

American continent

The American continent in general has little to offer European aviation archaeologists, who would be better advised to go east than west. The territory is vast, making travel, let alone transport of salvage, impracticable. Also, aerial battles have rarely taken place in American skies so that there are few areas where wrecks are likely to be concentrated.

South America

The South American republics are of particular interest as operators of veteran military aircraft, several of the republics still operating aircraft of World War 2 vintage. However, enthusiast organisations in the United States are well aware of this and have made bids for many of the aircraft. In fact, some American companies dealing in scrap metals have negotiated for the aircraft purely for sale to enthusiasts.

The whereabouts of the World War 2 aircraft are too well documented now to merit investigation, but some older items of aeronautica may well exist. Since the end of World War 1, military aircraft have been acquired by these republics and some parts, particularly propellers, are likely to have survived. For example, of the only British designed operational monoplane of World War 1, the Bristol Monoplane, 12 (C4929, C4982-4989, C4991-4993) were supplied to Chile. There have been a number of good articles in aeronautical magazines, particularly *Air International,* on air forces and their equipment over the years. One of the best books on the subject is *The Air Forces of the World,* by William Green and John Fricker, published by Macdonald in 1958.

There is a known area of wrecks from aerial combat in South America; a result of the almost forgotten and little documented war between Bolivia and Paraguay, fought 1932-35 over the Gran Chaco. Aircraft types involved were Curtiss Falcons and Hawks, Junkers W34s, Potez XXVs, Fiat CR30s, Caproni Ca 101s, etc. But the snag is that the Gran Chaco is a vast thick jungle area.

The United States

American enthusiasts are much too well aware of the interest in veteran and vintage aircraft to leave any earth unturned in their recovery; teams setting out from Europe might well be viewed as poachers rather than fellow enthusiasts. While the majority of Americans indulging in aeronautica are as enthusiastic as their British counterparts, aeronautica has become far more commercialised than in Britain. The first of the large auctions of veteran and vintage aircraft was held in June 1968 at Orange County Airport, California, when 29 aircraft including a DH4, SE5A, Nieuport 28, Pfalz DXII and Fokker DVII were on offer. Many were bought for museums and the top price paid was $40,000 for a Sopwith Camel that went to a Manhattan stockbroker. Because of the great number of enthusiasts in the United States, the lack of really old aircraft, the competition for aircraft and aeronautica and the lack of a national organisation for preserving aircraft, a new trend is developing. In the same way that ordinary antiques are being bought up by Americans, so are Americans now seeking aeronautica in Britain for two reasons — to maintain the veteran aircraft they hold and to acquire new items both as enthusiasts and for their value. Americans are also looking, as mentioned earlier, to South America.

Canada

Another country with vast areas making both wreck discovery and salvage a major operation, Canada offers little for aviation archaeologists. Aircraft that went missing during World War 1 are still occasionally being found but over a very wide area. There were three main spheres of activity in World War 2, the East and West coasts and the training stations under the vast Empire Air Training Scheme. It would be possible to search for years and not find one wreck, yet wrecks are come upon purely by accident. On December 8 1972 a bulldozer on road work in woods 20 miles north of Chicoutimi, Quebec, came in contact with wreckage proving to be of Hurricane XII 5624 that went missing in a snowstorm on November 15 1943.

One area where there are several wrecks is Vancouver Island. Two Liberators and a Ventura wreck have been located in this heavily-timbered and mountainous terrain. The wrecks have been visited by University of Victoria officer cadets — under an adventure training scheme which in itself suggests the difficulties involved. New markers were made for the adjacent graves but no recovery was attempted.

One of the greatest finds in recent years was the remains of a Curtiss HS-2L built in 1918 and which crashed in 1922. It was salvaged for restoration in the late 1960s and in spite of lying in mud for nearly 50 years, some tools found in the wreck were still usable. But this salvage operation involved the use of Canadian Forces helicopters. This emphasises the point that any investigation of wrecks in Canada is best left to the Canadian authorities.

Wrecks in South-East Asia and Australasia

Many ardent searchers, feeling that British ground has been over-worked, have expressed the desire to search virgin areas of the Far East, feeling that areas must be scattered with wrecks of Allied and Japanese aircraft. On the six airfields on Singapore in September 1945, there were 258 aircraft abandoned by the Japanese. These were all completely destroyed as was any evidence of crashed aircraft outside these airfields. The same is true of Hong Kong and the New Territories. The object then was to completely eradicate any sign of Japanese occupation and the writer, who searched these areas in the mid- and late 1940s, can vouch for the thoroughness of the measures.

Singapore and Hong Kong are, of course, relatively small areas. The wrecks that do remain are mostly in the vast and inaccessible jungle regions of Burma and Thailand, and there they are likely to remain. The aircraft salvage operations in recent years in the Pennines, Norwegian fjords and the Zuider Zee have received much publicity in aeronautical magazines, for which reason they are not recounted here, but in South-East Asia it is different. The reports of the investigation and salvage attempts 1942-1948 are sufficient to deter all but a well-prepared expedition. The account that follows of the aftermath of just one operation gives some idea of what was done in the past to investigate wrecks in this area and the hazards involved.

Salvaging Jap aircraft

After a Japanese air raid on Feni, India, November 28 1943, a Japanese aircraft was reported shot down in Chittagong somewhere near Subalong, 170 miles south-west of RAF Base Camilla where a Repair and Salvage Unit was alerted to investigate. A party of four set out next day in two vehicles, travelling 100 miles over bad roads which brought them to within 40 miles of the crash. At ferries en route there were delays of up to four hours due to tides. For the next stage it was necessary to get a Royal Engineers' launch. This ran on to a shelving bank and turned over, throwing personnel, tools and kit into the muddy water. The kit floated away and took time to recover and the tools could not be seen. A sorry party retreated to a bungalow known to exist at Rangamuti. Tools were irreplaceable in the Far East at that time, so the Superintendent of the Chittagong Hills Tract Police was contacted for grappling irons, but all that was recovered was a battered hurricane lamp.

On December 2, by a lucky stroke, an RE unit was contacted in the vicinity and lent tools. One of the party with two native police guides set out to walk through the jungle to the crash a mile away — which took three hours. It was found to be an Oscar 2 in a badly crashed state. Next day the party worked at the site, buried the Japanese pilot and dug the engine out of the ground. Photographs were taken and some engine parts and two 12.7 mm machine-guns were taken back.

While returning, a runner reached the party to inform them that another enemy aircraft had descended near Dighinala. There were no roads, only a jungle track by which it would take some four days to reach. They were advised by the District Commissioner to take elephants, which were ready by December 8 and proved to run at about 18 miles per day. At night they had their forelegs tied together to prevent escape, but which allowed sufficient rein for them to forage around, and they ate for most of the night. Two of the party were bruised when a howdah slipped off and one had a tick bury itself in an armpit which had to be killed off by a lighted cigarette end.

Getting nearer to the crash, a native policeman contacted the party, bringing in two machine-guns, a pistol and nameplates which indicated a Lily. The policeman led them to the site which was reached on the 12th. Only one engine was visible, the other being buried completely and was only found after a long search. This was dug up and parts removed. It was suspected that many parts had already been removed by natives and a police search of the area netted a parachute, oxygen bottles and a number of nameplates.

In mid-December instructions reached the party that RAF Intelligence wanted the Oscar engine salvaged — but by that time it had sunk into the mud. To haul it out and convey it back to Camilla, some 50 coolies were hired. A tree was felled and a 20-foot length of 10-inch diameter served as a cradle to which the engine was tied and which 25 coolies could move — with the other 25 acting as relief. After stages by boat, and eventually by van, the party struggled in with the engine on Boxing Day to be told that there were six more sites for attention.

This will give some idea of the difficulties to those who contemplate searching new areas. First the permission of the Governments of Bangladesh and Burma would be necessary. Hiring elephants, boats and porters would be involved and this story illustrates that the heavy units like engines tend to sink deep in the soil and will go deeper with succesive monsoon periods. Fuselages will have been ransacked. As for bringing parts of airframes out, government officials are not fools. They know that a party prospecting for minerals in their territory would not go to all this trouble except for the most valuable of minerals, so you must expect to pay a levy equal to its weight in gold!

The writer knows of three stalwarts who frequently brave rainstorms in the Pennines and Snowdonia in winter. They once boasted that no site is too difficult for them to tackle. Boys — Bangladesh, that's the place for you.

Investigating Allied aircraft wrecks

Once the war was over there was no further interest in Japanese wrecks, but there were a number of Allied aircraft still just reported as missing and, with only the elements to battle, these were investigated.

The War Crimes Investigation Teams and Army Grave Concentration Units had fed much information back to the Air Ministry on aircraft that had been missing during the campaign which included areas of Siam (Thailand), Indo-China (Vietnam), the Netherlands East Indies (Indonesia) and Burma. It was difficult country, with valleys of impenetrable jungle and few tracks. Also in the monsoon period, from May to September, torrential rains turned dry streams to raging torrents, and plains and valleys became vast lakes, making tracks impassable and destroying graves and scattering wreckage.

In December 1945, HQ Air Command South East Asia reported that there were still 300 aircraft and 1,000 airmen unaccounted for. To trace their fate, Nos 1 - 5 RAF Search Teams were established in Burma, each comprising an officer, senior NCO and airman driver, with Jeep and trailer. All were volunteers and mainly aircrew who had flown over the territory. After jungle training the teams set forth in February 1946 operating from Mandalay, Meiktila, Rangoon in Burma, and from two locations in Indo-China.

It was a long job, thwarted at times by monsoons, the need to hire boats and repatriation of team members. No 5 Team eventually cleared the Arakan between February and May 1947. At this time, to speed up work new teams were formed, No 6 to cover the Central Irrawaddy, No 7 the Upper Irrawaddy, No 8 from the Irrawaddy Delta to near the Salween River and No 9 in the Imphal and Kohima area. All Burma teams were withdrawn in August 1947 having located or collected information on some 250 wrecks.

The teams were strictly investigation and had no means of salvage which would then have been pointless. The reports on the location of the aircraft should be generally available to the public by 1978 for any expedition or, if anyone is feeling particularly adventurous, there are some 50 still unlocated wrecks of RAF aircraft assumed to be in the west and north-west of Burma and Bangladesh.

Two new teams, Nos 10 and 11, were formed in May 1947 to comb Malaya, allotted to the west and east coasts respectively. The teams, both based on Kuala Lumpur, set out in June and came chiefly upon the wrecks of Blenheims, Vildebeests, Hudsons and Buffalos from the fighting over five years before. However, much preliminary work had been done by Army teams in 1946 and one team was sent up to Thailand to investigate areas not covered by No 4 team.

HQ South-East Asia later in 1947 issued a summary which stated that further investigations in the Far East would be a waste of time, and that Burma, Siam, Malaya and Indo-China had been covered as far as was humanly possible with the time, personnel and equipment available. This in itself is a warning that the area is hazardous and costly for any enthusiasts to make any general expedition, but wrecks reported by local civilians do occur from time to time. In 1962 villagers near Mersing reported a wreck and a party from RAF Seletar at Singapore set out up-country to investigate and identified it as Brewster Buffalo W8202 of No 21 Squadron, Royal Australian Air Force. The pilot had forced-landed after a collision on January 12 1942 and, unhurt in spite of extensive damage to his aircraft, he had spent six days in the jungle before being found by an Australian Army patrol.

Australasia

Australia is far too vast a country for there to be any wreck areas, apart from isolated finds, except in the Darwin area which has been well searched. Most Australian enthusiasts have been looking further north to New Guinea, one of the centres of activity in the South-West Pacific Theatre of World War 2.

One of the leaders in this field has been Geoffrey Pentland of Kookaburra Technical Publications. His underwater salvage of a Japanese Zero fighter is one of the epics of recovery. The Zero now stands in the Central Science Museum in Tokyo where it has pride of place. A remarkable and encouraging thing about this item was the extraordinary good state of preservation of the Zero in spite of years in sea water and augers well for further salvage.

The Solomon Islands became a centre to several parties in the late 1960s. These included an Australian expedition in 1968 to the crash site on Bougainville of the Mitsubishi G4M Betty in which Admiral Yamamoto was shot down. No salvage or even souvenirs were taken. Around the same time a Corsair was found in a native garden on the island. A Canadian expedition to the surrounding islands found four Japanese aircraft which were taken by barge to Port Moresby and airlifted to Canada.

During the 1950s there were still dumps of American-built RNZAF aircraft of World War 2 in New Zealand, and one type, the Harvard, has remained in service to the mid-1970s. However, by the 1960s the NZ Aviation Historical Society was actively searching and in 1971 they rediscovered the wreck of a Hawker Hind abandoned in the Tararua Mountains and have attempted salvage. But throughout Australasia, most salvage jobs are for expeditions — not just enthusiasts.

Identifying finds

When a wreck or pieces of wreckage are found, a primary task is to find the identity of the aircraft concerned. With a complete aircraft it is possible that its identity number may be revealed, but more often it is a matter of deduction. Most aircraft parts, even bolts, bear markings, and from a relatively small piece of wreckage nationality at least can usually be deduced. Markings and plates may reveal a manufacturer and certain component markings indicate a type. Helped by local information on date of crash, the possibilities are narrowed until finally all details will correspond with details of a missing aircraft to provide the final link. But to do this you need to know something about markings and what they mean. Also, beware of 'red herrings'; servo-motors, fuel pumps, etc, may all bear nameplates and serial numbers. These items may be common to several different aircraft types and their serial numbers bear no relation to the identity of the aircraft.

Airframe identity markings

For any British Service aircraft the positive identification of any individual aircraft is the serial number allotted when the aircraft was ordered and which, with very few exceptions, remains the airframe number throughout service. The system of numbering dates from 1912 with the Army and Navy taking up blocks of numbers in a 1-10,000 range, followed by a series prefixed by letters A, B, C, etc, in a 1-9999 range for RFC, and later RAF, aircraft. An exception was naval aircraft with an N prefix from 1916. From K onwards the range was reduced to 1000-9999 so that all serials had a five-character identity, a rule that still appertains. Numbers were allotted consecutively until 1936 when blocks of numbers were omitted as a security measure. After Z9999 was reached in 1940, two letters were used, AA, AB, etc, to AZ, followed by BA, BB, et seq, in a reduced range of 100-999. Today the allocations reach the ZA, ZB, etc, series. The number is normally marked on the rear fuselage and is known as the serial number.

Certain numbers are not used, such as 'O' to prevent confusion with 'D', and there have been other anomalies over the years. The listing of serial allocations by aircraft types was given in the Patrick Stephens publication *British Military Aircraft Serials* of which this 5th edition gave allocations 1911-1979.

The unit an aircraft served in may be revealed by code letters. The British system 1938 to 1950 was to allocate two letters to units which were, on occasions, changed. These were marked on the fuselage sides one side of the roundel, balanced on the other side by the individual letter of the aircraft within its unit. The most complete list of unit codes published was contained in *Squadron Codes 1937-56* by Michael J. F. Bowyer and John D. R. Rawlings, published by Patrick Stephens in 1979.

Civil aircraft of any nation are identified by registration letters of which the initial letters are indicative of the country of registration. A complete list of British registrations allotted to aircraft types 1919-1970 was published by Ian Allan in 1970 — *British Civil Aircraft Register,* by Gordon Swanborough and John W. R. Taylor.

United States military aircraft (USAAF and later USAF) bear their identity markings near the cockpit. These markings consist of two letters relating to the American fiscal year in which the aircraft was ordered, followed by the number allotted to the aircraft in sequence in that fiscal year; the two numbers being separated by a hyphen. A slightly abbreviated form of the number is normally given in larger figures on both sides of the vertical tail surfaces. The numbering system, with its anomalies and changes over the years, manufacturers' codes and type and sub-type designations, is well explained in the Putnam series book *United States Military Aircraft Since 1911,* by Gordon Swanborough and Peter M. Bowers. While the book does not give a straight numerical listing of USAS/USAAF/USAF allocations as a guide to types, it does give the serials allotted by aircraft type. A similar reference is given for US naval aircraft in the companion work *United*

States Navy Aircraft since 1911, which covers serial and unit marking systems as well as detailing serial allocation by types. More recently the Merseyside Aviation Society has produced a listing of US Navy serials 1941-76 and USAF serials 1946-74.

But the fact must be faced, evidence of the serial number will rarely be found in wreckage. It is usually a case of trying to deduce a type from markings on small pieces.

Engine identity numbers

Engine identity numbers are more likely to be found than the serial marking on the airframe, which tends to crush like a shell on impact, whereas an engine, as a fairly compact mass of metal, is much less likely to break up. An engine plate with its type may well be found, but there is no record, published or even existing, of engine numbers, let alone linking them to the aircraft to which they were fitted. The airframe record cards and accident reports may quote engines fitted, but to find the aircraft type from the engine number in this way is like being given a seven-digit telephone number and trying to link it with a name in the London telephone directory. Another factor is that one particular engine may be fitted in succession to several different aircraft, so that a tracing back to the original installation record, does not confirm the airframe identity at the time of a crash.

Engines normally have two identity numbers, the maker's sequence number and the official recording number. To give typical examples or World War 1 engines circa 1916: 80 hp Gnome No 20864/WD41 (Avro 504A); 80 hp Gnome No 3825/WD42 (Henri Farman 7441); 90 hp Curtiss No 848/WD6850 (Curtiss JN4); 70 hp Renault No 33/WD356 (MF Shorthorn A2456); 90 hp RAF No 22986/WD1019 (BE2c 4171). In this case the WD — War Department — number was the official identity and the first number the maker's number. The high numbers are due to the fact that, while the design firms might number their engines from No 1, a contractor, making the same type of engine, would number from say, 10,001, and a second contractor perhaps from 20,001. The Hispano Suiza firm had 20 contractors in six countries, each with different blocks of numbers.

An 'A' prefix was used in 1918 in place of the former WD number but this was later dropped and British aircraft engine identities were normally just the two numbers; examples are given for the famous Lancaster III PA995 in early 1945 when it had completed over 100 sorties: Merlin 38 15485/250481 port outer; Merlin 28 7947/326756 port inner; Merlin 28 3338/267357 starboard inner; and Merlin 28 6518/325802 starboard outer.

Assembly markings

Large assemblies of British aircraft were normally marked with their manufacturers' part number stencilled, together with the nature of the surface finish as a guide for repair. Finishes were given by their DTD (Directorate of Technical Development) specification number. The part numbers often bore prefix letters indicative of the manufacturer. Examples are as follows: A3 — A. V. Roe (Avro); AS — Airspeed; EEP — English Electric, Preston; F8 — Fairey Aviation; G5 — Gloster Aircraft; MCO — Morris Cowley, Oxford; PAC — Percival Aircraft Ltd; PPA — Miles (Philips

& Powis); PSC — Pressed Steel Company; SFR — Rootes, Speke; TAY — Taylorcraft/Auster; VABH — Vickers Armstrong, Broughton; VACH — Vickers Armstrong, Chester; 41H — Hawker.

This coding is a guide to the manufacturer, not necessarily the type, due to extensive sub-contracting. EEP, for example, built Hampdens and Halifaxes and MCO Tiger Moths. But it is not just the odd marking, but by the examination of a variety of parts that a picture can be formed of the aircraft concerned. However, the system can be complicated, as it was a compound system. Typhoon Ib MM955 under repair at Marshall's in 1945 bore a panel marked TAY/R/PSC/G5/21453, which indicates that Taylorcraft (Auster) repaired (R) the panel manufactured by Pressed Steel Company (PSC) on Gloster-built (G5) aircraft with a panel assembly number 21453.

British aircraft component identification

In recent years most of the famous names of aircraft manufacturers like Avro, Blackburn, Fairey, etc, have disappeared in mergers. But, as far as the majority of British historic aircraft are concerned, they were built by famous firms in World War 1 that were still producing aircraft in World War 2 to drawings numbered in a series that remained unchanged over the years. The various numbering systems used by each company would be too involved to include here in detail, but a general survey is possible.

The part numbers marked on each component were the drawing numbers which the Air Ministry decreed would be marked on all components where practicable. Some had prefix letters indicative of the firm, such as SB for Short Brothers. Some numbers broke down into parts with the initial digits the aircraft type number, the following digits the number of a main assembly, and the final digits a part number within that assembly.

Major components bore manufacturers' plates with serial numbers of the component — not of the aircraft. The aircraft's own identity number was, apart from the serial marked on the rear of the fuselage, normally marked on the main fuselage bulkheads and/or on the main formers of the wing centre-section.

Inspectors' stamps appeared on all components where practicable. These were of two types, AID and AID Approved, The Aircraft Inspection Department (later Directorate) was formed on January 2 1914 and each inspector was allotted a number which was preceded by the letters AID. Works inspectors, approved by the AID, had stamps with a separate num-

Items of aeronautica — **left** *a Spitfire tail trimming tab scroll plate used as a teapot stand and* **right** *a pilot's rescue whistle circa 1944.*

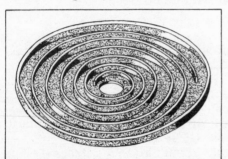

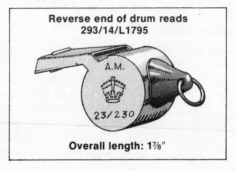

Reverse end of drum reads
293/14/L1795

A.M.

23/230

Overall length: 1⅞"

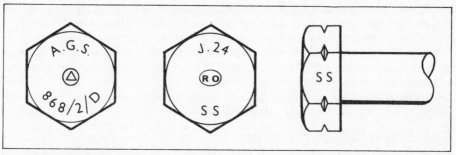

AGS bolthead codings.

bered series for each firm, prefixed by letters significant of the firm. These are often a good guide to the aircraft firm, but again it should be appreciated that there was extensive sub-contracting.

AGS parts

Thousands of small aircraft parts on British aircraft — bolts, studs, fork ends, clips, etc — were, and still are, AGS (Aircraft General Standard) parts which bear no relation to any particular aircraft type. These standardised parts were planned at the Royal Aircraft Factory, Farnborough, during World War 1 with numbers 101 to 500 for various items, eg 101-112 to types of hexagonal bolts. For dismantling for renovating parts it is useful to know that AGS bolts and screws are all right-hand threaded, so that you turn anti-clockwise to undo them. The markings on the boltheads represented various factors — for example in 764/4/E the 764 would represent the material specification, the 4 and E a coded reference to bolt diameter and length respectively. Some had a simpler system, eg J24, where J was the code letter for diameter and the number was the length in tenths of an inch.

German component identification markings

Unlike Britain, where old established aircraft firms of World War 1 were each conducting part numbering systems of their own, German planning in the completely reconstituted aircraft industry of the early 1930s decreed a common numbering system that would be used by all German firms producing aircraft for the Government. It was bound up with the Luftwaffe designations for aircraft types in a simple numerical series prefixed by an indication of the design firm, eg Ar-Arado, He-Heinkel, Ju-Junkers, etc, hence Ju 88.

The part numbers had a qualifying material category number, eg 8 Airframe parts, 9 Engine and propellers, 10 Safety equipment, etc. This was hyphenated to the aircraft type number, eg 8-111 would indicate airframe part of a Heinkel He 111. A further suffixed number would relate to an individual part, eg 8-111-075432 in which 07 was indicative of an assembly and 5432 the individual part. Most large assemblies had makers' plates attached with date of manufacture. On the outside of the aircraft, and in the cockpit, would be the final assembly plates giving the Werke Nr (the aircraft's identity number), contractor (more aircraft were built under sub-contract than by the designing firm), date of completion and full type designation. From wreckage, it would appear that it is easier to establish the individual identity of a German aircraft, than a British; but it should be appreciated that under the German maintenance system, overhauled and salvaged parts were often sent to aircraft production units for incorporation on new aircraft. An interesting facet of their radio equipment was the use of coloured bolts and screw heads to indicate which parts could, or could not, be disassembled for maintenance. A more detailed survey of German aircraft component numbering is given in Appendix E.

Piping identification markings

Colour coding of piping was introduced on British Service aircraft in 1916 with coloured bands at intervals along the piping of all systems, and on each side of every joint. Codes were as follows: petrol — red; compressed air — yellow; oil — black; water — blue; pressure pipe of pitot tube — white; air service pipes of petrol system — yellow and red.

The RAF extended the scheme and piping in World War 2 aircraft was marked as illustrated:

RAF standard piping code.

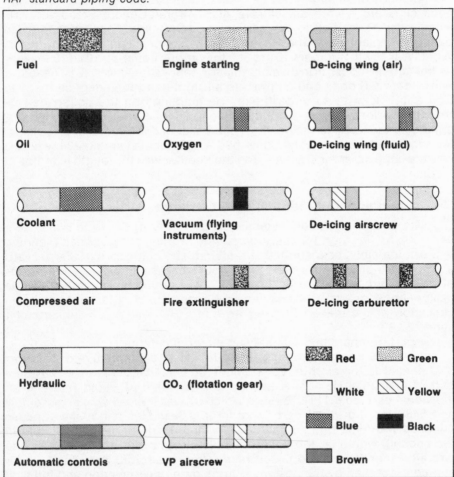

A standardised piping coding was introduced on American aircraft early in the 1940s as follows: fuel — red; oil — yellow; coolant (water) — white; coolant (glycol) — white/black/white; compressed air — (low pressure) light blue, light green; (high pressure) yellow, light green; hydraulic fluid — light blue/yellow/light blue; oxygen — light green; vacuum — white/light green; fire extinguisher — brown; flotation gear — light blue; de-icing — white/red; smoke screen system — brown/white; air speed indicator pressure — black; air speed indicator static — black/light green; boost pressure — white/light blue; steam — light blue/black; exhaust analyser — light blue/brown; vent (closed compartment) — red/black. Some American aircraft were built to British contracts in which British coding was specified, but this did not normally apply to Lend/Lease aircraft which had American piping markings.

RAF equipment code

Soon after the RAF was formed a stores referencing system was introduced and, where practicable, this was marked on the equipment and/or its container. From 1926 the Air Ministry Crown, with the letters AM, were also marked on stores items, as the equivalent of the War Office's WD (War Department) stamp used on RFC equipment.

Stores were divided up into various ranges of equipment, allotted, initially, numbers from 1 to 100. These numbers give a clue to wreck investigators of the type of equipment found which may not be obvious from distorted fragments. Some of the main ranges are: 5 electrical equipment, 6 navigational and optical instruments, 7-9 various items of armament, 10 communications equipment (initially W/T only), 11 bombing gear, 14 photo and projection equipment, etc. Each range was broken down as necessary into sections, eg while the 12 range was armament, 12A items were bombs, 12B dummy bombs, 12C ammunition, 12E torpedoes and associated equipment, 12F miscellaneous armament fittings, 12G fuses, etc. Within these ranges, parts were numbered from No 1. Thus in range 25 propellers, of which complete units were numbered in section 25A, a Tiger Moth propeller, being the 399th type of propeller in RAF use, would have the stores reference 25A/399.

In general, stores were items common to all aircraft, but one range does give a clue to type identity, which might well be useful in identifying wreckage. This was Section 26 concerned with airframes and special-to-type fittings in aircraft.

RAF stores code marking as on bridge-piece of pilot's goggles, 1944.

The sub-sections were coded according to the aircraft type, eg 26C Ripon, 26D Iris. Other suffix letters related as follows: E Fury, F Vimy, G Wapiti, J Whitley, K Bulldog, L Nimrod, M Cloud, N Southampton, P Audax, Q Tutor, R Sidestrand, S Vildebeest, T Hyderabad/Hinaidi, V Hart, W Demon, Y Flycatcher (later Harrow) and Z Virginia. Double or treble letters were also used as follows: AAA Hector, CC Hinaidi II, CCC Gladiator, DD Dart (later Anson), GG Rangoon, HH Tomtit, JJ Battle, PP Avro 504N (later allotted to test benches), QQ Gauntlet, SS Victoria, TT Moths (all types), VV Horsley, WW Siskin, YY Gordon/Seal/IIIF and ZZ Atlas.

From the late 1930s the special-to-type equipment was prefixed 26A with a further letter denoting the type, eg 26AC Blenheim, 26AF Hurricane, 26AH Botha, 26AJ Spitfire, 26AK Henley, 26AL Sunderland, 26AM Hampden, 26AN Oxford, 26AS Magister, 26AR Botha, 26AS Mentor, 26AT Wellington, 26AU Lysander, 26AV Lerwick, 26AW Bombay, 26AX Manchester/Lancaster, 26AY Beaufort and 26AZ Defiant.

The next series of allocations were 26BA Halifax, 26BE Fulmar, 26BF Stirling, 26BG Harvard, 26BH Hudson, 26BJ Master/Martinet, 26BK Albemarle, 26BL Whirlwind, 26BN Proctor, 26BP Beaufighter, 26BQ Queen Wasp, 26BS Tornado, 26BT Barracuda, 26BV Vega Gull/Q6, 26BW Dominie, 26BX Typhoon, 26BY Mosquito and 26BZ Firefly. The allocations 26C and 26D were reserved for the miscellaneous types of impressed aircraft, eg 26CP Moth Minor.

Late World War 2 aircraft parts were in Section 26E as follows: 26EA York, 26EC Warwick, 26ED Horsa, 26EF Hengist, 26EJ Welkin, 26EN Auster, 26ER Tempest, 26EW Hornet, 26EX Messenger, 26EZ Buckingham, followed by early post-war aircraft allocations, 26FA Brigand, 26FC Vampire and 26FD Spiteful.

With Lend/Lease equipment of World War 2, the same section numbers were used with 100 added, so that where 10H was used for British communications equipment, Section 110H identified American communications equipment. In the special equipment to type, Section 26, Lend/Lease aircraft types were identified as follows: 126HA Baltimore, 126HB Kittyhawk, 126HD Tomahawk, 126HE Airacobra, 126HF Boston, 126HG Buffalo, 126HH Bermuda, 126HJ Vigilant, 126HK Catalina, 126HL Liberator, 126HO Lightning, 126HP Maryland, 126HQ Mustang, 126HR Fortress, 126HT Vengeance, 126HU Goose, 126JH Lodestar, 126JJ Argus, 127JL Mitchell, 126JM Marauder, 126JP Mariner, 126JQ Dakota, 126JR Thunderbolt, 126JV Coronado, 126JZ Hadrian, 126KB Ventura, 126KC Piper Cub, 126KE Hellcat, 126KF Helldiver, 126KG Cornell, 126KH Expeditor, 126KL Hoverfly, 126KM Nash-Kelvinator helicopters, 126KN Sentinel, 126KQ Sikorsky YR-5A, 126KS Douglas DC-4 (Skymaster), 126KT CG-13A gliders.

AERONAUTICAL ARCHITECTURE

When the American Forces came to Britain during World War 2 and established the Eighth and Ninth Air Forces in Britain, they likened the country to a vast aircraft carrier. Certainly in eastern and south-eastern England, airfield almost skirted airfield.

Even in World War 1, there were several hundred airfields located in the British Isles, ranging from stations with more than a hundred aircraft on strength, such as at Cranwell, to just a landing ground for a detached flight of a Home Defence squadron. All entailed some alterations or installations and even more so in World War 2. As a result, there are some thousand sites in the United Kingdom that have evidence of wartime aeronautical activity.

World War 1

The Royal Flying Corps, when formed in May 1912, had a standard form of permanent hangar: a large wooden shed with gabled front and sliding doors to house up to three BE type aircraft. In later years some of the wood was replaced by galvanised iron and several examples of these original structures remain at various early airfields. One at Manston is in use as a store by a merchant. This is not exceptional. They were based on the galvanised shedding used by the British Army to accommodate garrison stores in the outposts of Empire. For example, some shedding sent to India was trans-shipped to South Africa and erected during the Boer War — and it still stands!

With the great expansion of the RFC in 1916 came the 1917 pattern hangar, examples of which can be seen at a dozen stations; Duxford provides a typical example, and one such hangar was incorporated into the construction of the Royal Air Force Museum. They were designed to accommodate the aircraft of a training squadron, and were built in groups of three to four to form Training Depot Stations. A full census of these structures, surviving aircraft sheds and hangars of the 1914-1918 War has not apparently been published and this is a field of original research that can be done, combined with a pleasant country holiday. Many farm sheds of today were housing aircraft 50-odd years ago.

Canvas endures

For use in the field, particularly on the Western Front, canvas hangars were used. At first there were two main types. The RAF (Royal Aircraft Factory) hangar designed in 1913 was. 53 feet wide, 43 feet deep and 19½

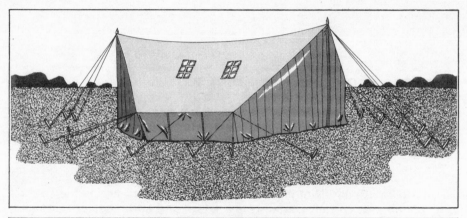

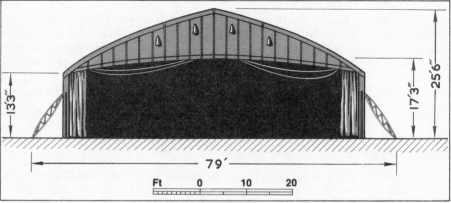

Top *RAF-type canvas hangar, 1914 and* **above** *Bessoneaux canvas hangar.*

feet high at the centre. This was soon superseded by the RE7 type, of 60 × 38 × 20 feet respectively, because that was of lighter, simpler construction and thereby more portable. It is doubtful if any remain, but of the Bessoneaux canvas hangars that followed on a large scale from 1916, some are still stored by the RAF for emergency use today.

The Bessoneaux hangars were 66¼ feet deep. A series of Hervieu hangars were introduced from 1917, some with 130-foot spans to accommodate HP V/1500s and to meet requirements of the Independent Air Force. Now you, in the 1980s, may well enter one — for the Army has one it uses still to house exhibitions, although its aeronautical significance is apparently not appreciated.

Properly treated and stored, canvas is a very strong and durable material. Canvas hangars were camouflaged in various ways suitable to the terrain, and from June 1918 were delivered dyed dull myrtle green.

Railway links

There is an airfield link for the railway enthusiasts, who are fascinated in tracing disused railway tracks. During the 1915-1919 period there were standard gauge lines serving Cranwell from Sleaford, a distance of five miles, while Manston had a line from Birchington and from Thetford sidings there were lines serving the airfield. At Calshot the flying boat station had a narrow gauge railway put down in 1917 which operated for 30 years.

World War 1 airfields and bases

Apart from the abandoned airfields of World War 2, which constitute a feature of the landscape in parts of the country, there is still evidence of over a hundred World War 1 airfields or bases in the British Isles. At a number of locations the original aeroplane hangars or sheds still stand, in a few cases the airship sheds still exist and seaplane slipways, and balloon sheds are also apparent.

The smallest of the WWI airfields were the Landing Grounds (LG) for which ground was usually rented, levelled and maintained. At these fields the minimum was a hut with a telephone and a store for pyrotechnics and equipment. Some landing grounds were greatly expanded as Home Defence (HD) airfields and so became, in the parlance of the times, aerodromes. Some of the largest of the World War 1 aerodromes were the Training Depot Stations (TDS). These housed a grouping of normally three Training Squadrons and were bases for squadrons mobilising for overseas. Normally large brick hangars were built in clutches of three, of which Duxford provides a fine example; the hangars there were built in 1917 for training squadrons which became No 35 TDS in July 1918. Base aerodromes were those at Aircraft Acceptance Parks (AAP) where aircraft built in regions of the country were tested for service acceptance, and the Aircraft Repair Depots (ARD) which salvaged and rebuilt aircraft.

Coastal stations, which were mainly operational, often had both airfield and a seaplane (SP) station, and sometimes also an airship station. The trend in late 1918 was towards landplanes replacing floatplanes in antisubmarine operations.

Typical World War 1 airfield layout.

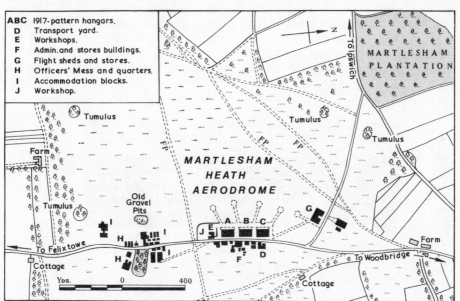

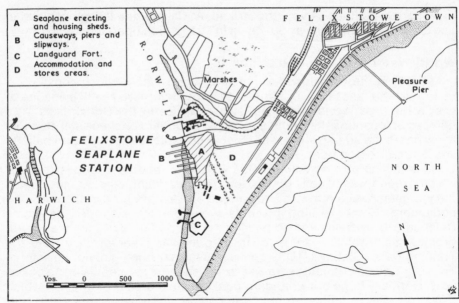

Typical World War 2 seaplane station layout.

As the airfields/bases were named after the parish in which they were situated, location is not a difficult matter once you have a name. A list of 1914-18 airfields and air bases in the British Isles is given in Appendix A.

World War 2

Between the wars, the RAF stations were mainly wartime stations placed on a more permanent basis with, for example, brick administration, guard-room and messes replacing wartime wood and iron structures. But the 1917-pattern hangars remained, some to be destroyed in the German attacks on bases during the Battle of Britain, while others stand today.

From 1935, under successive RAF expansion schemes, numbers of airfields were built around the country. Operational bomber airfields had to be sited within reasonable striking distance of the Continent where the

C Type hangar, end view.

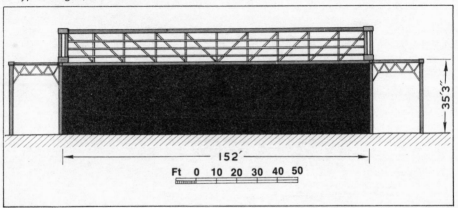

threat from Nazi Germany was growing. New coastal airfields sprang up around the country and training airfields where the conditions of level ground, good drainage, reasonable weather record and road access appertained.

This intensive building continued unabated for ten years, 1935-45, controlled by the Air Ministry Works Department at a thousand different sites to support the air effort of the Allies. Various contractors were called in and airfields were also built for the United States Army Air Force as well as American formations taking over former RAF stations during the 1942-45 period.

Architecture of the expansion period

During the expansion period 1935-39, the airfield buildings were mostly of brick for permanent use, and to facilitate rapid building a number of set designs were approved for hangars, barrack blocks and messes. Building blocks were, in general, restricted to two floors and were built in well proportioned Georgian style, with brick and tile colour appropriate to the locality. At Hullavington, for example, stone facing work was incorporated to conform with the Cotswold district of Stanton St Quintin. In spite of the urgency, the designs were subject to the approval and review of the Royal Fine Arts Commission, and the views of the Society for the Preservation of Rural England were sought where appropriate. The handsome bonus for the taxpayer is that, as a result, these are in the main the buildings that are today housing the Royal Air Force.

Recognising hangar types

At any airfield, it was the hangars that dominated the scenery. The old 1917-style hangars had been supplemented, prior to the expansion, by structures of similar style giving a clear span of 120 feet width, being 250 feet long with high doors each end 25 feet high. These dimensions distinguish a pre-1935 curved-roof hangar and they became known as Hangars Type 'A'.

For the airfields of the expansion period a new style hangar was designed, known as Aeroplane Shed Type 'C', roofed by a series of 12 gable sections which, from a distance, appeared as a flat roof giving the

D Type hangar, end view.

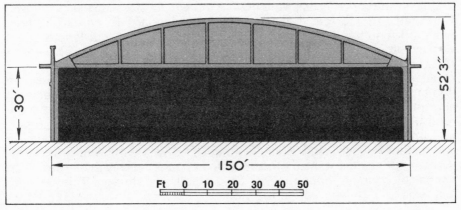

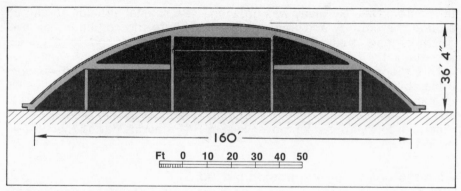

E Type hangar, end view.

150 feet wide by 300 feet long and 35 feet high (inside clearance) structures a box-like appearance. They were steel-framed with bricking to
match the rest of the station's buildings. Early examples in the expansion
period were Bassingbourn, Benson, Brize Norton, Cottesmore, Dishforth,
Driffield, Finningley, Hemswell, Honington, Hullavington, Leconfield, Linton, Scampton, Shawbury, South Cerney, Upwood, Wattisham, Watton
and West Raynham, all of which retain examples of expansion period
building. In the same way that the 1917 Type A hangars became the general aircraft-housing buildings of the post World War 1 years, so have the
expansion period hangars remained the general hangars of the RAF today.

For the war period, eight other types of hangar appeared for various
purposes. 'D' Type hangars for aircraft storage units were of reinforced
concrete with a 150 × 150 feet floor space and 30 feet clearance to the roof
which was arched. Many examples of these exist at former maintenance
depots. To meet changing conditions and supplement the needs of stations rapidly growing in size, 400 Bellman transportable hangars were
produced 1938-40 and a few examples of these may not only be seen on
current and disused airfields, but transported to factory sites far away from
any airfield. They can be identified by size, 95 foot span, 180 feet long and
25 foot door height. Their original corrugated iron sheeting covering, over
the steel framework, has in some cases been replaced by other materials.

After the Bellman came 906 'T' type hangars, officially called a transportable shed, built 1940-1945 to designs by the Tees Side Bridge &
Engineering Works. These were built in three main sizes, spans as follows:
T1 95 feet, T2 115 feet (became known as standard T), and T3 66 feet.
Standard length was 240 feet and door height 25 feet, but length could
vary according to special requirements. Like the Bellman, the Ts were of
steel construction, covered with corrugated iron sheeting.

But the most numerous hangar type of all was that used on wartime
fighter and trainer fields, the 3,000-plus blister hangars for single small
aircraft. Many examples remain. These too, were of three types, the standard 45 feet-wide ribbed wooden arch and the 65 and 69 foot steel arches,
all with corrugated iron covering and canvas doors at each opening, 45
feet distant in each case. Some were covered with earth and grass grew
over for concealment. Also blister-like in appearance was the large E-type
hangar of concrete construction, used chiefly for storage. This was 160
feet wide and 34 feet high at the centre.

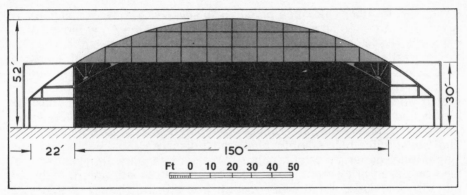

K Type hangar, end view.

Runway tracing

In general, hangar size and shape did not greatly differ between World Wars 1 and 2, but the great difference was on the field itself. Aircraft weights had increased greatly and both runways and hard-standings were necessary; the danger from bombing meant dispersal of the aircraft around the field necessitating a perimeter track, bomb-pens for the aircraft and shelters for personnel. It is vestiges of these that appear all round the countryside.

The longest runways were of 4,000 yards for emergency landings, but a standard bomber airfield had a main runway 2,000 yards long — well over a mile — and 50 yards wide, built on a north-east/south-west facing, with two others in different directions 1,400 yards long of similar width. Other stations had smaller runways and in all 444 airfields had runways laid in the United Kingdom during World War 2. Others had Pierced Steel Plank (PSP) as a temporary arrangement. Now partly overgrown, these numerous airfield sites, particularly in East Anglia, can still be traced out.

Airfield domestic sites

The stations of the expansion period had much to commend them; the associated married quarters were constructed at a period also noted for the quality of workmanship and the barrack blocks (built to accommodate

T Type transportable shed.

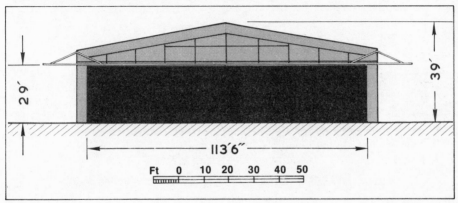

52, 68, 78, 94, 102 or 126 men plus four to seven NCOs) were spacious by Army standards. Small wonder that in recent years the Army moved in to places like Bassingbourn and Waterbeach when the RAF gave them up. For the interest of Service personnel who now live in them or use the messes — and this concerns thousands — their original condition is reviewed.

Up to 1935 most barrack blocks had either scrubbed floorboards or brown lino-covered concrete floors. The new post-1934 RAF barrack blocks had hardwood flooring, chiefly Jarrah, which was highly polished. This proved rather noisy and rubber or linoleum strips were later supplied. The walls, with their smooth plastered finish, were painted in various single tone, generally bright, colours. Walls of sanitary annexes were of tiled or glazed brick and fittings were of a more refined pattern than had hitherto been used for the Services. It is gratifying to record that in a general report on RAF buildings, after their intensive use throughout the war when blocks held far more than they were designed for, that many of the original fittings remained. Perhaps they still do.

Airfield hutting and shedding

Up to 1938, building was largely to meet an enlarged permanent air force, but after that it was to complete stations for a state of war which was becoming imminent. Already a brick shortage had conditioned a general change from brick to concrete construction. At some stations hutting was acceptable for accommodation and 'spider-blocks' were erected through-out the country. These raised wooden huts were built in two rows of three, interconnecting with a bricked ablution and latrine block. Each spider could comfortably accommodate 150 men. Other hutted accommodation, mostly to standard Air Ministry drawings, but built by local contractors, was intended to last, at a maximum, 15 years.

Dilapidated hutting may still be seen around many airfields and many huts have been removed after sale or from other means of acquisition to various locations, particularly to smallholdings. The standard Air Ministry Type A hut was a product of the expansion scheme. These are still a popular acquisition for the stout timber frame was covered by sheet asbes-tos roofing, cedar weather boarding walls, and lined with fibre or plaster-board. They were built in 18 and 28 feet widths and, having wood flooring, they could easily be moved. Type B, also erected 1935-39, differed by

Officers' Mess entrance, expansion period in pseudo-Georgian style.

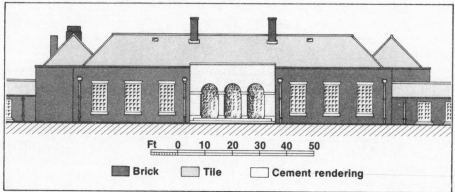

Ft   0   10   20   30   40   50

■ Brick   □ Tile   □ Cement rendering

Nissen hut, end view.

board roofing. For wartime airfields and expansion on existing stations, Air Ministry Types X, Y and Z prefabricated huts were standard erections on the growing and dispersed domestic sites. Basically to the design and construction of Type B, they were in various lengths to a standard 18 foot width — the ideal to accommodate two rows of beds or bunks with a central aisle.

The most familiar of huts is the Nissen hut used in both World Wars, but when re-introduced in World War 2, in early 1941, the flooring was almost invariably concrete. Several other hut types were erected on the Nissen principle, which was basically semi-circular steel rib frames, spaced at roughly six foot intervals, covered with corrugated steel sheeting. Normally there was a form of wall boarding inside. These were built in 16, 24 and 30 foot widths and could be extended to any length, the standard being 36 feet, with extensions in multiples of six feet. Each end was made of brick or wood, with a door and two windows one end. Similar in shape, introduced mid-1942 were Everite and Handcraft huts, both 36 × 18 feet, but produced in asbestos cement sheeting, troughed on the outside and flat inside.

Easily confused with Nissen huts were Romney and Iris huts. From the outside they had a similar appearance, but were 35 feet wide and built in bays of eight feet. Internally they can be distinguished by the ribbing which was tubular; they were used mainly as stores. Marston 35 × 45 foot sheds of corrugated steel sheeting over a light steel frame were erected for garages and stores throughout the war.

Two small types of concrete buildings mushroomed around airfields in the mid-war years. The Ministry of Supply Maycrete hut of 1941 had reinforced concrete posts with Maycrete slab walls and a board and felt roof and was 16 feet wide by 54 feet long. The larger Ministry of Works Orlit hut of 1942-43 was 18½ feet by 60 feet of similar construction, but had a pre-cast concrete roof.

Looking back today

Old airfields abound. Some of the old buildings are being used, appropriately, for the housing of veteran and vintage aircraft. Apart from the World War 1 hangars used by the Imperial War Museum at Duxford and the RAF Museum at Hendon, several private organisations are using buildings on abandoned airfields for preservation work and exhibition. Other old airfields are used by gliding clubs, some have been left to the ravages of the elements but are otherwise untouched, while others are being made into building sites or restored to agricultural land. Much of aeronautical interest remains to be explored and researched — and not only on old airfields.

Exploring old airfields

In the late 1960s, there were still murals and even pin-ups on the walls of huts in disused airfields, and at one airfield visible chalk marks on an operations board. Now, in the mid-1970s, the weather and vandalism have taken their toll, but there is still the airfield layout to measure up and explore.

Airfield archaeology could make an interesting school class project. Both fieldwork and research is involved. The background history will start at the local library; the indices of bases in standard books like *Bomber Squadrons of the RAF*, by Philip Moyes, or *Fighter Squadrons of the RAF* by John D. R. Rawlings, may well give leads to the units stationed at the airfield so that a picture of the station's operational role is built up. If the airfield was opened pre-war, the library files of old newspapers might well be fruitful, but do not expect too much of wartime references because of censorship.

Local residents may have billeted airmen or worked at the airfield, and local interviewing might be rewarding. Do not expect too much of people's memories when it comes to dates. Information can be sifted and cross-checked later.

Fieldwork, after having permission of the landowner, involves exploring and mapping. First the runways should be paced out to orientate the map to be made, and then the dispersal track traced to set the initial bounds of the flying field. This will give some idea of size to decide on a scale. An allowance should be made for 1,000 yards in all directions outward from the dispersal track for ancillary sites.

As related earlier, hangar and hut types can be largely classified and dated from their dimensions and styling. Uneven ground may reveal bomb shelters, dispersal pens and the butts. On wartime-built airfields, the living sites were at least 250 yards from the administrative and technical buildings around the hangars, and a WAAF site even further removed. In south and south-eastern England there may well also be airfield defence sites still visible. Gradually a picture can be built up of the area as it was. It will reveal the great upheaval that occurred during the war years bringing more changes to the countryside than any other event in the past 1,000 years.

In the same way that disused railways have produced some interesting studies in flora and fauna, so is the same true of disused airfields where a thin topsoil over concrete has brought wild flowers foreign to the surrounding district. Since concrete runways have, in many cases, been the obstacle to the return of the land to agriculture, wildlife abounds. There is certainly a place for those with a biological bent to participate actively in a disused airfield study project.

The toll of war was not restricted to operations. Almost as many aircrew were killed in accidents as by the enemy and most accidents occurred landing or at take-off and thereby on or in the vicinity of the airfield. The headstones on the graves of local churchyards may well have evidence of the toll of war. And several churches near airfields had steeples damaged by aircraft!

Round and about

It is not only on airfields that buildings will be found with aeronautical connections. After World War 1 a spate of wireless masts and stations appeared, usually at some distance from the airfield to avoid masts being a hazard on the landing circuit. Then there were the small wooden huts that were once dotted far and wide at the centre of four tall masts. These were the MF/DF (Medium Frequency/Direction Finding) stations that gave position fixes to aircraft. The first stations opened at Worthy Down, Eastchurch and Mount Batten, but the first two were re-sited at Bircham Newton and Andover. During World War 2 these were expanded and 26 were in operation. They were active throughout the war giving bearings to returning bombers and reconnaissance aircraft, notifying Air Sea Rescue of SOS calls and homing lost night fighters. They had a place post-war until September 1958 when the last went out of service on the introduction of more sophisticated equipment, such as automatic triangulation. The masts were dismantled and so were most of the huts, but a few of the latter remain in use as shepherds' huts, a sports store and a henhouse, but who now recognises them for what they were, or realises the drama enacted within their walls? For those abandoned on site, there may also be vestiges of the landlines by which they were all interconnected.

Around the English east and south coasts is a chain of Martello towers, circular forts built early in the 19th Century as defences against threatened Napoleonic invasion. They are the subject of many books and objects of great historical interest and, incidentally, some were adapted for various purposes in World War 2 for stores and observer posts. But what of the defences around the coasts against the Nazi invasion? Here is a new field of re-discovery, and limited sectors can be investigated during a seaside holiday. There were the CHL (Chain High Low) radar tower sites, some still with concrete standings, anti-aircraft battery positions, Royal Observer Corps posts (there's a plaque on the one on top of Beachy Head), even the occasional coastal airfield or landing ground, perhaps even the vestiges of an airship station, such as just off the coast road between Dover and Folkestone at Capel.

Project hometown

The effect of air warfare can be traced in many of our large towns, particularly London, Manchester, Coventry and Liverpool that suffered in the Blitz, by an architectural study. The fine new city centre of Plymouth is due entirely to the devastation of war making building anew necessary; the same goes for Coventry's fine new cathedral. But apart from these famous examples, there remains evidence of wartime bombing at several thousand sites spread over the country.

There is not a London Borough without tangible evidence of the suffering of its people during the war in the architecture of the surburban streets. The rows of terraced houses with the gap, perhaps filled with a house of more modern design and sometimes a series of filled gaps along or across rows of houses, where a Dornier or Heinkel unloaded a stick of bombs. There are the larger gaps, areas flattened by the V1 and V2 weapons, now with blocks of flats.

An interesting series for a local newspaper, that could be submitted as a school project, would be a 'then and now' series. Most borough central libraries and archives will have civil defence records with maps of incidents. Pictures may be held at the Imperial War Museum (apply by letter for permission and appointment to peruse photo records) to illustrate the 'then' and pupil photographers could illustrate the 'now'. Such a project can, of course, be considered as one aspect of a general 'hometown in the past' project.

Further projects

A comprehensive book has yet to be published on airfields in Britain, although it has been researched and in particular by the Airfield Group of the Air-Britain organisation. The subject is so vast that if a comprehensive history was given for each airfield, production costs would be very high. On the other hand a breakdown into regions would have limited appeal. But a school or society project of this nature would be breaking new ground and may greatly interest an editor or a local paper, and gain a small reward for school or society funds.

It would have been helpful to have given within the confines of this book a background to the airfields that can be found, but with a thousand fields, some with a history of over 60 years, it would take several volumes. The field is wide open.

There is room, too, for a book on airfield names alone, to link places like Heath Row and Squires Gate, to the places they serve (ie London and Blackpool) and to find the origin of RAF airfield names. It has been the policy to name service air stations after the parish in which they are situated, intriguing names like Kingston Bagpuize, Kirton-in-Lindsey, Stoke Hammond, etc, occur. There are Cornish airfields with the inevitable 'tre', 'pol' and 'pen' in their names, Saxon elements like 'tun' or 'ton' (Ossington, Oulton, Ouston, etc, to name but a very few), 'ley', meaning an open glade in a wood (eg Finningley), 'wick', a dairy farm (eg Hardwick) and, of course, 'ham', an enclosure or village has been the name ending of more than 50 RAF stations.

Following World War 1 many civil airfields were opened; this is a further line that can be pursued. These fields required Air Ministry licence and some, Category D3, were very confined and labelled as suitable only for 'Avro 504K and similar types'. Examples are the sands at Seaton Carew; Derby Racecourse; Uckington, Cheltenham; West Blatchington, Brighton; Trent Lane, Nottingham; Chapel Hill, Margate; Brean Down, Weston-super-Mare, etc. This opens a further line of research for, being at a time when wartime censorship was no longer operative, locations can be consulted in the aircraft periodicals of the period, *Flight*, *Aeroplane*, *Aeronautics*, etc, which can be perused in the larger central reference libraries.

Aeronautical memorials

Memorials to aviators abound, ranging from individual headstones in country churchyards to international edifices like the Commonwealth Air Forces Memorial at Runnymede on which are the names of all Commonwealth Air Force personnel who lost their lives flying on operations in the UK and NW Europe and have no known graves. There are memorial windows in cathedrals and headstones or plaques at outlandish places marking the sites of crashes. Several people have been involved in recent years in cataloguing aeronautical memorials and a guide-book may result, published by an association if not on general sale.

One of the most impressive memorials is that to the Lafayette Escadrille, the American volunteers who flew with the French in World War 1. This large, semi-circular shrine, with crypts containing the remains of men of the escadrille, is at Garches, just west of Paris. However, to enter, it is necessary first to make prior arrangements with the caretaker.

There are memorials in many RAF station churches and chapels, but these are not always open to the public; but the Central Church of the RAF in the Strand, Central London, is open to all. A church is believed to have existed there since the 9th Century and the building to Sir Christopher Wren's design was destroyed by enemy action in 1941, leaving only the walls and steeple standing. The church, fully restored and re-dedicated in 1958, is maintained by private charity and devoted work.

There is the famous stone behind Dover Castle marking the historic spot where Blériot landed in 1909, after making the first cross-Channel aeroplane flight. The RAF Memorial and Trenchard's statue can be seen along the embankment between Charing Cross and Westminster and many famous aviators are commemorated at airfields and airports. Finally, there are the many roads and buildings named after famous airmen. Aviation has a very broad association with architecture.

READING, WRITING AND RESEARCHING

Aeronautica is an interest, generated by information, which leads us to seek more by books, magazines, records or correspondence. The more we read, the more knowledgeable we become; but since our reading is rarely guided or planned, a block in our comprehension can occur. Often we miss out on basic information, for most writers in books and magazines assume that the reader has some basic knowledge of the subject. This must be so, or books would be too repetitive if every technical term was explained.

Here we assume the reader is new to the field of aeronautica and guide him gently into the realm of aeronautical publications and records, help him to understand the official records that provide the opportunity of original research and, both for the novice, and the enthusiast of standing, ways of recording and writing are suggested, and some of their pitfalls explained.

Delving into aeronautics

There are three main ways of delving into the history of aeronautics; reading published works; being a member of an enthusiasts' organisation and so qualifying for their restricted circulation specialist publications; or perusing original official documents and reports.

Published works

Practically any published aeronautical book is available for you to peruse, if you are prepared to wait, under a national library scheme. Your local library may have a limited selection of aircraft books, but application can be made for any title (quote author and publisher if you can) under a national book interchange scheme for the local council's stipulated fee for book reservations.

Aeronautical magazines abound — the technical and commercial weeklies, the enterprising fortnightly and the professional, technical and the enthusiasts' monthlies. The ones of your selection can be subscribed for annually, be bought from your newsagent by reservation or casual purchase, or perused in the larger of the reference libraries.

Magazines are less popular than books for research because of indexing and storage difficulties. They can be bound up like books and many magazine publishers have binding schemes, but this does add to costs. Most magazines deal very broadly with aeronautics and a particular reader may only be interested in a small percentage of the content; also it is often cluttered with pages of advertisement. As a result magazines are often cut up; the articles of interest are torn out and the rest discarded — this creates another, but less bulky, storage problem which we will come to later.

Association publications

Membership of an organisation will give access to publications not available through booksellers, although some second-hand shops do trade in these publications. Members of the Royal Aeronautical Society enjoy not only a highly professional journal monthly but exceptional library and research facilities of their own. As mentioned elsewhere in the book, the 661st issue of their *Journal* in January 1966 is one of the best aeronautical historical works in existence. But the society is, of course, restricted to professional people with certain qualifications.

There are many organisations for aero enthusiasts, both on a national and regional basis. Your membership will be welcomed for the usual membership fee which varies, but is normally under £5, and for this you receive their periodic publications. These usually contain items that would not have sufficient appeal to warrant inclusion in a national aeronautical periodical, for example aircraft wreck sites, a listing of the serials of every aircraft of a certain type and what happened to each one, airfield logging reports and special articles. Since these organisations are normally non-profit making and have an Hon Secretary and Hon Sales Manager (ie unpaid) they give very good value for money.

The prime aircraft enthusiasts' organisation in this country is Air-Britain, the International Association of Aviation Historians, who claim to be the oldest and biggest, all-voluntary, world-wide aviation interest movement, having 2,850 members in 55 countries. Members enjoy a periodic digest and news, and an information service by specialists on many aspects of aeronautics. Photos, registers and monographs by members of the organisation are offered at privileged prices. At time of writing the Hon Registrar will send particulars on receipt of a request including return postage. The organisation advertises in the aeronautical press and has a particular association with Air Pictorial.

The American Aviation Historical Society claims that their *Journal* (available only to society members) is the leading aviation historical publication in the world today. Printed on deerskin opaque, a high-quality semi-gloss paper for good photographic reproduction, and containing upward of 72 pages per issue, it certainly is the best produced enthusiasts' magazine in the world. Annual dues of $ 20 include a newsletter as well as the *Journal* which has appeared quarterly since 1956. As would be expected, the content is mainly on American aviation, but there is good coverage of units based in Britain and of American aircraft in British service.

For World War 1 enthusiasts there are both American and British editions of *Cross and Cockade* journal, another quarterly. The quality of these publications has to be seen to be believed. The accuracy of contents, originality of features, and high standard of reproduction, put many commercial magazines to shame. Subscription is currently £8.00 payable to the Membership Secretary, Mrs. Christine A. Chinnery, 23a Winchester Street, Farnborough, Hampshire GU14 6AJ.

Keeping records

Storage of books is a simple matter of bookcases, the main difficulty is space. With a host of periodicals on the market and association publications abounding (Air-Britain alone have been producing specialist sheets and monographs since 1948), papers begin to pile up. How can this mass of paper be kept in good condition and easily accessible? Most people accept that periodicals have to be discarded over a period, papers of interest being extracted. This presents a filing problem of method and system.

Enthusiasts speak loosely of their files. The basic file is a folded cover, the stiffer the better, containing papers grouped by subject or period. Papers easily spill out so that it is usual to have them secured with an Indian Tag piercing the top left-hand corner. This means that the papers are all bunched together at the top so that, since some papers are shorter than others, there is an unequal spread and the files do not lie easily one on top of the other. The easiest storage pattern is to stand files on end like books, but this has two drawbacks — the weight of the papers bearing on the tag at the top tends to bow the file and break down the stiffness of the cover, and there is no spine on which to title subject matter for ease of reference.

There are various ways of filing and some business organisations have some sophisticated methods, that can be both expensive and expansive. The best compromise to give a reasonably efficient filing system at modest expense, taking the minimum of space, is the wallet or pocket folder. The papers being enclosed do not need tagging. The weight of the papers then bears on the gusset at the bottom resting on the shelf, and the folds (or gusseting) in the edges provide a flat spine for labelling the contents. These pocket folders, about 10p each, can be purchased in a variety of colours so that you can plan your own colour coding, eg red for aircraft firms, green for aircraft types, blue for personalities, etc. A 13 × 9 inch folder will take the contents of most magazines without folding.

As files grow, so there comes the storage problem and shelving becomes necessary. Pocket folders are larger than outsize books so bookcases are rarely suitable. Shelving, racking or filing cabinets need to be used. Make-up shelving is currently marketed, but this can be expensive as it is designed as furnishing. For attic, den or cupboards, boxes or strong cartons can be adapted. A lateral support is needed for files every 18 inches — taking 25-30 files — as a long shelf or rack of files will flop and become too heavy to be easily handled. The sheer weight of paper should not be underestimated. A year's *Airfix Magazine,* for example, will weigh over 4 lb, some reference books even more. Your storage must have firm supports and beware of making it top-heavy. Because of the weight problem wall shelving is not recommended, massed paper needs strong base support. The floor should be examined first for dry rot and woodworm — falling racks loaded with paper could crush and cause fatal accidents.

Official records

The source records are the official records. Commercial publications give the opinions of writers who may merely have culled the facts from earlier books and may not have consulted basic records at all. You may wish to exercise your privilege to see what was documented at the time on the subject of your interest. From the better books you have perused you will be aware that much documentation must exist and be available to some, but to what degree can you expect records to have been made and kept and how can you see them? This is explained.

RFC/RNAS records

The records of the Royal Flying Corps and the Royal Naval Air Service were meticulously documented. Most aspects of aircraft at war were the subject of reports, operational accounts were given in communiqués that detailed even the precise number of rounds fired and photographic plates exposed per day, progress on experimental projects was given in fortnightly reports, aircraft dispositions and production progress reports appeared monthly and there were masses of correspondence. Many of these records have been preserved.

Unfortunately there has been some spillage. A few valuable records appear to have been lost. It has to be accepted that some unit records went up in smoke by enemy action, accident and arson. One omission appears to be the aircraft built up from salvage; there are a few files preserved that detail every turnbuckle changed on a couple of Farman Shorthorns, but the types and numbers of aircraft built up at repair and salvage depots have apparently escaped the net. Records of Training Depot Stations and Training Squadrons are by no means complete, and the ledgers of naval aircraft taken on charge and their subsequent service records, tagged for permanent preservation, were destroyed by a later reviewer.

Prime records of the RAF

In the immediate post-WW1 years the RAF set out the responsibilities of Commanding Officers in keeping records; hitherto joint Admiralty/War Office systems had been followed. Over 40 books were to be kept by each unit; some were of little historical significance, casual payment and messing accounts, but included were aircraft, engine, marine craft and MT vehicle log books, one for each of these items held, also a watch log by flying stations. Unhappily, few of these have survived.

Historical records for squadrons and other units have fortunately been preserved in practically all cases. This record is often referred to as the 'O-R-B' or 'Five-Forty' because the details were entered on RAF Form 540 to make up the Operational Record Book. The object of this document was to furnish a complete historical record of the unit or headquarters from the time of its formation. ORBs were introduced in the mid-1920s and most units included retrospectively at that time, a summary of the previous history of the unit/squadron. The subsequent entries vary greatly according to the recording officer who was advised to consider entries daily. Changes in location, function, organisation, equipment and command were considered relevant, but the Air Council's advice of 'Any other matter which may be considered of historical interest' was liable to wide interpretation. Unfortunately it was stipulated that events occurring in the normal course of peace-time duty were *not* to be recorded. As a result participation in the annual air exercises, practice camps, competitions and flying displays usually went unrecorded and so another gap in our historical records occurs.

In war the regulations for completing the 540 were much more rigorous, weather conditions, badges or devices authorised, decorations and promotions all had their place in the book. Also, another important historical document was introduced as an appendix to the 540 for inclusion in the book. This was Form 541 Detail of Work Carried Out, for use during operations only. This detailed times, crew, aircraft, load and target, for every operational flight, successful or abortive, so that in general a brief can be found on every single sortie during World War 2.

All this is but a fraction of the World War 2 records. There are Fleet Air Arm records but in a rather different form of logs. There are all the Air Publications — the handbooks on aircraft, engine, marine craft and mechanical transport types, armaments and instruments, training techniques and procedures, historical studies and surveys. There are Command intelligence summaries detailing our own and enemy action day-by-day for the various theatres, operation reports, monthly statistical surveys running to a hundred or so pages, Command activity reports, Air Ministry Orders and thousands of files. At the time the Air Publications were officially classed Restricted, many other documents were Confidential, the ORBs were all Secret and some files Top Secret. Over the years these have been downgraded in their security classification, Unclassified being the official term for documents now open. Also, under current legislation, official information can, in general, become public information and released to the Public Record Office after 30 years. In the case of the RAF operational records the Ministry of Defence taking over the Air Ministry has not caused any difficulty, but other aeronautical records are not so straightforward.

Experimental and production aspects were administered by the Ministry of Munitions which, post-World War 1, became part of the Air Ministry which shed these branches to a separate Ministry of Aircraft Production, later absorbed in the Ministry of Supply, that became the Ministry of Technology and subsequently split, part going to the Ministry of Defence as the Procurement Executive. Don't blame the archivists if some of these records have become split!

Public Record Office (PRO)

The PRO is open from 0930 to 1700 Monday to Friday, except on public holidays and around the first two weeks of October when there is annual stocktaking. It is situated at Ruskin Avenue, Kew, Richmond (Telephone: 01-876-3444), where there is a large car park, and Kew Gardens London Underground District Line station is nearby. Visitors must have a Reader's Ticket, obtainable at reception provided that you certify your identity, with a passport for example. The ticket number at the top left, less prefix, is of importance for it must be quoted on all applications for perusal. Items such as bags and coats have to be deposited in a cloakroom, and a visitors' book signed. If you have a typewriter with you, tell the officials, who will arrange special accommodation.

It is advisable first to get a bleeper, so that when your documents have been traced you can be alerted. This also bears your allotted seat and desk with a letter guide to the area of your seat. In the reference room you will find the index files. A leaflet on the ranges can be obtained from the officials, who are both knowledgeable and helpful. The air records have references preceded by AIR and these main headings are detailed in Appendix F.

After selecting items to your maximum allowance of three, you feed their references into a computer which has instructions for its operation. Should there be a computer breakdown, yellow request forms have to be filled in. A short wait follows during which one can have refreshments downstairs or, at certain times, a meal. Your bleeper will give out its note wherever you are in the building, but not in the car park, where these devices should not be taken anyway. The average time taken to find a document is about 20 minutes, although this may be extended. On the sounding of the bleeper and its accompanying flashes, the reader goes to the distribution counter and quotes the seat and group number, say 34F, and is then handed the document. If loose-leaf files are involved, these are only issued one at a time as a precaution against an accidental mixing of the contents.

Very occasionally one is disappointed by a requested document failing to be issued. This is because it has been reserved by a reader to have photocopies made. This is happily rare but it does happen and extraction from this department is virtually impossible, as while they are there, these documents are identified by an order number and not by index number. There may be a time lag of five days before a document is returned to the normal shelves, but when a backlog builds up it can be considerably longer. A charge is made for photocopies requested, and the counter dealing with this work is through the automatic doors to the left of the distribution counter.

An additional service provided by the Public Record Office is that of supplying aircraft drawings or maps for examination. For these, go to the map room on the second floor.

No documents or other records are available for inspection before 30 years have elapsed after the date of the last item entered. There are, however, exceptions listed and displayed in the Reference Room.

Readers should remember to return their bleepers to the Distribution counter before leaving.

All in order

Some of the basic records that can be perused, covering every facet of administration, discipline, dress, equipment and activities, are the Service Orders. Up to the formation of the Royal Air Force, many administrative matters for the RFC and RNAS appeared in the respective Army and Admiralty Orders, but there were specialist orders for the two air arms — Air Technical Orders for the RFC introduced in 1917, and the earlier Technical and Gunnery Memorandum for the RNAS. With the formation of the RAF these were discontinued and two new series of orders were introduced — Air Ministry Weekly Orders and Air Ministry Technical Orders, the latter being replaced in the 1920s by Equipment Orders. Following the pattern set by the Admiralty and the War Office, these orders were numbered from No 1 annually and were always quoted by year, eg AMWO 106/19 would be the 106th Air Ministry Weekly Order issued in 1919.

Each order might vary from a line to several pages and each has a short title as a guide to content. To give a typical example, AMWOs 784-799/20 promulgated September 9 1920 for 'information and necessary action' by the Air Council concerned: 784 — Outside Looping; 785 — Meteorologist

Airmen; 786 — Extension of Service and Re-engagement of Airmen; 787 — Rates of Exchange; 788 — Loss of Discount on Gas Accounts; 789 — Danger Zone on French Coast; 790 — Inland Area Golf Meeting; 791 — Gosport Speaking Tubes for Flying Training Units; 792 — Disposal of Vehicles; 793 — Prices of Aviation Spirit and Oils; 794 — RAF Flying Manual PT II; 795 — Excessive Demands for Stationery; 796 — Re-introduction of Title GOC-in-C in certain Army Commands; 797 — Forms and Publications based and re-numbered; 798-9 — Amendments to Kings Regulations. It will be seen that many orders concerned domestic matters of the RAF, but a close perusal of these orders over the years reveal many interesting facts and figures that will not be found in any published book.

These orders were reorganised at the end of 1930. From January 1 1931 the main orders were split into three series. Equipment Orders, which dealt mainly with modifications to airframes and engines, continued for a time, but after a few years the bulk of these were incorporated in the appropriate airframe and engine Air Publications (basically handbooks) with periodic updating amendments. The AMWOs were split into separate Administrative and Temporary series, each numbered from No 1 per year and prefixed respectively by A and N to identify the series. The administrative A series included such subjects as camouflage and markings of aircraft and vehicles, but the introduction, nomenclature and withdrawal of main items of equipment, aircraft and engines, appeared in the N series. These two series continued throughout World War 2, and provide a valuable guide to changes in organisation, dress, badges, correct nomenclature, aircraft, marine craft and vehicle types, radio equipment, etc.

Air Publications

The handbooks of the RAF on Administrative and Equipment matters were the Air Publications, issued from 1918 numbered from No 1, and which continued right through World War 2. The books varied largely in style as well as content, some being thick bound books while others were flimsy large format soft-covered booklets. Selective examples are: AP120 — Handbook on the Vickers Gun; AP163 — Royal Air Force Trumpet Calls; AP595 — Rigging Notes DH9A; AP1182 — Parachute and Personnel Safety Equipment Manual; AP2513 — Gun Turrets for RAF Marine Craft; AP2656 — External and Internal Finish of Aircraft.

APs were kept updated with periodic amendments and were re-issued as necessary after the passage of years. AP129, for example, the RAF Flying Training Manual, when issued in 1920 with cockpit diagrams of such aircraft types as the DH10, Short 184 and Sopwith Snipe, bears little relation to the AP129 post-World War 2, so that when requesting some APs it is advisable to quote the year of your interest. Ideally, the year of issue should be quoted, but this may not be stated in some library catalogues. Another complication is that some APs comprise several volumes, each dealing with different aspects of the main subject, identified by suffix letters allotted alphabetically.

Included in the AP series are the handbooks on the various types, for example AP1363 Virginia, AP1381 Sidestrand, AP1573 Hart, AP1721 Beaufighter, AP2380 Avenger, AP4301 Dragonfly. A letter prefix was allotted to the AP number for subsequent issues covering later marks, the Spitfire I

Above *World War 1 rebuilds and replicas are all the rage among American light aircraft enthusiasts. Early in the field was this re-built Curtiss JN4 'Jenny' seen at Van Nuys in 1965, restored as an Air Service Mechanics School machine of Kelly Field (photo via Herb Kelly).*

Below *The Royal Air Force, proud of its history, has a Memorial Flight at RAF Coningsby, Lincolnshire, of four Spitfires, three Hurricanes and Lancaster all in flying condition, maintained largely by voluntary work. Shown is a Hurricane II and a Spitfire XIX (MoD PRB2947/4).*

Above *One of the many aeronautical museums in the United States, the Naval Aviation Museum at Pensacola, Florida. A restored Curtiss N-9 of 1918 in foreground and behind it (left) a Curtiss A-1 replica (US Navy 1160657).*

Below *Markings are all indicative. Where markings are evident, unit and approximate year can be deduced. The serial number at the rear of the fuselage, on checking with a serial guide, will show this aircraft to be a Hurricane Mk I of the first production batch. The code letters, on reference to the appropriate books or recent* Airfix Magazine *articles, indicate No 79 Squadron pre-war. Reference to camouflage and marking books show this roundel style on the fuselage side to be circa 1939 (via Brian Lowe).*

Above *Salvaging a Spitfire off Malta, 1973 with the co-operation of an RAF sub-aqua club. Although the engine was complete the aircraft had broken up and engine identity, as is explained, does not give aircraft identity* (Joint Services Public Relations Office, Malta).

Below left *Despite 31 years beneath a Norwegian lake, the cockpit of this Halifax bomber (see next page) is remarkably well-preserved* (MoD).

Below right *Component assembly markings as seen under the elevator of this Hawker Fury, Empire Day 1937. Markings show the serial repeated, the 41H Hawker prefix and assembly number, CX for Cellon Scheme X fabric doping and the W/T bonding marking. Those with squadron badge and marking interests will know this to be a No 25 Squadron aircraft* (C. E. Sergeant MBE).

Above *The longest ever overland wreck trek, to a Blenheim lost in the Libyan desert, May 1942, with the Kufra Oasis the nearest location point, involving a 1,155 mile round trip from El Adem by Land Rovers of No 1 (Field) Squadron RAF Regiment in conjunction with an Imperial War Graves Commission request.*

Below left, above and below *In 1973 the world's last surviving Halifax — TL-S:W1048, of No 35 Squadron, was recovered from a Norwegian lake by a team of RAF sub-aqua enthusiasts. The aircraft crash-landed on the frozen lake in 1942 after an attack on the Tirpitz and later sank. After 31 years submerged, some of her lights still worked! (MoD).*

Above *Artificial lake at Pampisford, Cambs, seen in 1965 caused by Halifax LW206 crashing in a wood with full bomb load off the Newmarket road, September 3 1944* (N. D. Robertson).

Above left *Look up as well as down! Section of Wellington wing 70 feet up in a tree at Wandlebury hill, Cambridge, February 1971* (Steve Gott).

Left *Relic of the Peenemünde raid. August 18 1943 — engine mount of Lancaster JA851 of No 49 Squadron recovered off the northernmost point of Alsen Island, summer 1970* (J. Helme).

Below *Typical 1917-type hangar showing the large buttressed brick ends, wooden arch, and original doors replaced by metal sliding and folding doors for World War 2. Fairey Fulmar in foreground seen 1941* (RTP9638B).

Right Perhaps the most outstanding salvage and restoration operation of a World War 2 aircraft was that of the unique two-seat operational Zeke A6M2-21 used as the personal aircraft of the naval commander at Rabaul, Commander Tomoyoshi Hori — now a bank manager in Osaka. The staff of Kookaburra Technical Publications, led by Geoffrey Pentland, lifted it from a coral reef in the South Seas, shipped it to Melbourne for restoration and then forwarded it to Japan for permanent exhibition (Kookaburra photo).

Right Restoration work often involves complete replacement of the majority of components. Here Jack Canary surveys Sopwith Snipe E6938 that had a long history of film work between the wars, before tackling its restoration in December 1953. The Snipe is now exhibited in Canada.

Below Originally built as flight sheds at Farnborough pre-World War 1, in the original RFC permanent hangar style, these buildings have been used until recently as MT sheds. They were scheduled for demolition in 1976. This 1975 photo shows a Shackleton I making one of its last flights at Farnborough before leaving for preservation at Strathallan. Behind the bus can be seen branches of the famous Cody's Tree replica (RAE N4494).

Above *Another group of RAF servicemen stationed in Germany have recently completed the restoration of this Ju 52/3m for the Berlin Senat Transport Museum. The aircraft was originally built in Spain in 1944 and served with the Spanish Air Force until Lufthansa obtained it in 1965 (CPRO RAF Germany).*

Below *A favourite excavation site in the Cheviot Hills is the area in which USAF B-17G 44-6504 crashed in 1944. Since 1968 enthusiasts have visited the site whenever conditions were favourable, and a .50 machine-gun is among the relics recovered after much hard work (David Smith).*

handbook was AP1565A, the Spitfire II AP1565B. The first of the manuals to be reproduced commercially, *The Spitfire V Manual,* published in 1976 by Arms and Armour Press in association with the RAF Museum, was AP1565E. The title given is a little misleading as it is not the complete manual but the Volume I Maintenance and Descriptive Manual part of AP1565E which, like other airframe manuals, had a second volume with maintenance schedules, unit and major repair schemes and equipment leaflets, and a third volume containing extensive schedules of spare parts — much sought by aviation archaeologists for component identification. Nevertheless, the airframe construction, controls and pilots' notes are all included in the new publication. No 2 in the series is the Hurricane II and no doubt others will appear.

Pilots' notes were included as a section of the Volume Is of the aircraft handbooks and were also printed separately as AP(PN)s. Several publishers have HMSO permission to publish these commercially and current advertisements in the monthly aeronautical magazines give an idea of the range available. Towards the end of World War 2, to save the delay in issuing handbooks, which normally appeared after the aircraft was in service, the American manufacturers' handbooks, written in conjunction with the USAAF and USN, were accepted for British maintenance procedures and issued as APs.

There is a vast amount of documentation. Examples of all should be held in the Public Record Office and many APs are in the RAF Museum Library. Between the wars many APs were on sale through HMSO and occasionally appear in second-hand bookshops.

Combat reports

It was incumbent on all service pilots to submit a formal report on any encounter in the air with the enemy, and the vast majority of the reports are held in the Public Record Office. The combats by RFC and RAF pilots in World War 1 were reported on Army Form W3348, Combats in the Air. These foolscap sheets have headings as follows: Squadron, Type and Number of aeroplane, Armament, Pilot/Observer, Date, Time, Locality, Duty, Height, Result, Remarks on hostile aircraft and Narrative with space for several hundred words for the pilot to give his own account of the combat.

The World War 2 forms varied according to Commands. Unfortunately the Forms F used by Fighter Command did not have provision for quoting the type and serial of the aircraft flown; otherwise, they were generally similar to the forms of World War 1 with a large space for a general report of the combat.

Understanding official records

Before you peruse the official air documentation of the past, it is as well to have some idea of the system of official correspondence and the meaning behind the mass of initials and references. The references under which the subjects will be found catalogued in the Public Record Office bear no relation to the references of the original documents which have been re-

referenced for record purposes. Once you have found the subjects of your interest you will find the documents and related papers under their original references. You are back in the past.

Official correspondence

There are five main aspects to any official paper — subject, text, reference, authorisation (the official putting his signature to the paper) and the date. The official air records, like most governmental business, are contained in files. An official file is a series of related papers tagged together within a cover, bearing a name indicative of the content and a number allotted by a registry. Files were raised as new subjects arose and 'grew' as papers, incoming letters and copies of replies, were placed upon them. These enclosures were tagged on to the right-hand side of the open cover.

In many cases it was necessary for one part of a Ministry to refer matters to another part, or to higher officials, for comment. This internal work was called minuting and such correspondence within a Ministry (Air Ministry, Ministry of Munitions or Ministry of Aircraft Production) was carried out on minute sheets placed on the left-hand side of the appropriate file. Minutes might be lengthy, or just a brief, signed, 'I concur', and were usually handwritten. This means that to correctly follow events through from beginning to end, you must read a file *backwards,* starting at the bottom enclosure and bottom minute sheet, scanning through both as you work to the top enclosures. During World War 2 when the Air Ministry was widely dispersed into various London buildings and in the north, it was not practicable to send files to out-stations and minutes were often sent like letters, which will explain the mass of correspondence in the AIR files at the Record Office headed 'Loose Minute' — it means in effect an interdepartmental letter.

In general, and particularly so in the World War 1 records, it is not always clear who is signing and thereby responsible for initiating a course of action, but the form of signature is a guide resulting from an inverted form of snobbery. The lowest of the staff officers, an SOIII (Staff Officer Grade III) might well sign in full *J. A. Hamilton, Captain, RFC,* while an SOI or SOII might merely sign *J. A. Hamilton,* a Director might feel plain *Hamilton* suffices and the Chief of Air Staff would consider it *infra dig* to end his minute with more than a mere — *H.* Moreover, Chiefs of the Air Staff and Secretaries of State enjoyed another privilege, the exclusive use of coloured inks. Thus the penned comments of these great men stand out from among the rest of the correspondence.

Most documents (letters, loose minutes, reports, etc) bear an official reference. This is normally the file number on which the paper originated and the branch initiating the paper. In a typical reference A.254173/40/Ops 2(a) the initial A, which heads so many official papers on air matters, stands not for Air, but for Adastral — the house where the central registry raising the file was situated. Similarly, most aircraft and equipment files of World War 2 have references prefixed 'H' because the equipment branches were evacuated to Harrogate — much to the consternation of local residents who feared they would become a Luftwaffe target. The 254173 was the file number given by the registry and the 40 was the year the file was raised, *not* necessarily the year of the document. Many files of 1940 were still in use in 1944, but running into several parts, each dealing with a set period. The Ops 2(a) related to the part of the Ministry raising the file which leads us to organisation.

A Ministry must, of necessity, be broken down into administrative units and at all levels these had two titles — a formal title and a short title, the latter for use in internal addressing and referencing. The main departments of the Air Ministry at the beginning of World War 2 consisted of the Departments of the Permanent Under-Secretary of State for Air, Chief of the Air Staff, Air Member for Personnel, Air Member for Development and Production (whose department was soon to blossom out to ministerial status as the Ministry of Aircraft Production), Air Member for Supply and Organisation and the Director General of Civil Aviation (then a diminishing department). These were the formal titles, but these worthies had the respective short titles, PUS, CAS, AMP, AMDP, AMSO and DGCA, which would appear on documents they originated.

The departments were divided into Directorates or Divisions headed by a Director or Assistant Secretary and might be grouped under a Director General, hence the DG and D of so many short titles in references, eg DGP — Director-General of Production, controlling DAP — Director of Aeroplane Production and DEP — Director of Engine Production. Directors were normally at Assistant Secretary level for civil posts and Air Commodore level for Service posts. In turn, Directorates were divided into branches, designated by letters and numbers, eg the Director of Operations would divide the various aspects of bomber, fighter, coastal, etc, operations into branches — Ops 1, Ops 2, Ops 3, etc. Branches were headed at Wing Commander/Senior Executive level and were further divided into sections headed at Squadron Leader/Higher Executive Officer level designated in the form Ops 1(a), Ops 1(b), Ops 1(c), etc. A sub-section might be denoted by Ops 1(a)1 and Ops 1(a)2; this would be at the lowest staff officer level of Flight Lieutenant/Executive Officer. Nevertheless, letters might well be actioned and signed at lower levels on behalf of a branch.

In general, the initials in a reference are an indication of the level at which a paper originated. In the Ministry of Aircraft Production there were Controllerates headed by a Controller. Anyone resarching aircraft development will constantly come across references to CTD of World War 1, who was Controller Technical Department, Department of Aircraft Production, Ministry of Munitions; or CRD of World War 2, who was Controller Research and Development, Ministry of Aircraft Production.

Correspondence from RAF Commands can usually be recognised by the prefix letters to file references — BC for Bomber Command, FC for Fighter Command, etc. While individual aircraft were normally referred to by a serial number, it was usual throughout Coastal Command to refer to aircraft by the letter allotted by the unit to the aircraft together with the unit number, eg T/220 would be aircraft 'T' of No 220 Squadron. Since the permanent serial number was not used, it makes the tracing of individual aircraft extremely difficult in this Command's records.

The references of lower formations can similarly be identified from indicative letters and figures. Group HQ prefixes were usually in the form of the Group Number and the letter G, eg 41G for No 41 Group. Stations adopted indicative letters, eg DUX for Duxford, MDH for Mildenhall, etc, and squadrons had a system similar to Groups in which 66S would denote No 66 Squadron.

Abbreviations

Official papers were raised originally for a limited circulation to those to whom the many forms of abbreviation would be understood. It is not so easy for the uninitiated perusing the records today. To record them all in full would take a book the size of a large dictionary, but some of the most common are explained as follows:

AID Aeronautical Inspection Directorate. **ACAS** Assistant Chief of the Air Staff. **AL** (followed by a number) Amendment List. **AMO** Air Ministry Order. **AMWD** Air Ministry Works Department. **AOC/AOC-in-C** Air Officer Commanding/in Chief. **BF** (when followed by a number) Branch Folder or (when followed by a date) Bring Forward. **C** Controller. **C of A** Certificate of Airworthiness. **D** Director. **E1, E2,** etc, Equipment Branch Nos. **F1, F2,** etc, Finance Branch Nos. **GD** General Duties (main flying branch of RAF). **MA** (World War 1) Military Aeronautics (branch of War Office). **MAP** Ministry of Aircraft Production. **Min** Minute. **MT** Mechanical (*not* Motor) Transport. **MU** Maintenance Unit. **Ops** Operations. **OR** Operational Requirement (Specification). **Org** Organisation. **R** (as prefix to number) Receiver. **RD** (World War 1) Research and Design. **RS** Reserve Squadron (became Training Squadrons from May 1917). **RT** Radio Telephony. **S1, S2,** etc, Secretarial Branch Nos. **SA** (World War 1) Supply Aircraft (branch of War Office). **SAA** Small Arms Ammunition (eg .303). **SOC** Struck off Charge (ie no longer on unit inventory). **Spec** Specification. **T** (as prefix to number) Transmitter. **TDS** Training Depot Station (*not* Squadron). **TR** (as prefix to number) Transmitter/Receiver. **TS** Training Squadron (Reserve Squadrons prior to May 1917). **WD** War Department. **WO** Write-Off. **WT** Wireless Telegraphy (ie signal using Morse Code — not speech).

Crash categories

For the benefit of aviation archaeologists researching accident records, the abbreviations relating to aircraft accidents are explained. During the first two years of war, aircraft were categorised as follows: **U** No damage. **M** Repairable at unit. **R** Repairable but beyond unit's capacity to repair. And **W** Write-off, repairable or lost.

From 1941 to 1945, seven different categories were used as follows: **U** No damage. **A** Damaged but repairable on spot by nearest RAF unit. **AC** For repair by contractor's working party. **B** Damaged but repairable at Maintenance Unit or contractor's works. **C** Destroyed but of salvage value. **D** Burnt out but of salvage value. **E** Complete write-off and no value except metal salvage. (Missing aircraft were categorised E after 28 days.)

Signals code

Much of the operational communications was by signal — the service term for a telegram. All accidents were reported to the Air Ministry by signal, so background information an aviation archaeologist may require could well be in the records of a unit reporting an accident by signal. These were not dated in the normal way. Like telegrams the day and time only were important; if month or year was involved, then the communication did not warrant signalling. Dates on signals were in a form of code as follows: 071754Z deciphered would mean the 7th day of the month (07) at 1754 hours (5.54 pm) Greenwich Mean Time (Z). If it was British Summer Time then the letter suffix would be 'A', or for Double British Summer Time (a wartime innovation) 'B'.

In mid-1916, when BE2 aircraft variants formed the bulk of unit aircraft equipment, a special telegraphic code was introduced and they appear in signal messages as follows: BETUC (BE2c), BETUD (BE2d), BETUE (BE2e), BETUF (BE2f), BETUG (BE2g). When RAF 1B engines were fitted, as distinct from RAF 1As, B was added as the final letter, for example BETUD1B.

During World War 2 aircraft casualties were reported by a coding as follows: **FB** Accident or incident due to operational flying. **FA** Accident or incident resulting from non-operational flying and not due to enemy action. **FC** When it was not known whether a casualty was due to enemy action, FC for 'flying casualty' was used. **GA** Ground accident. This coding was also adopted in correspondence and records.

Punctuation in signals can be confusing to the uninitiated, as phrases in World War 2 were punctuated by CMA, CLN and PD which should be read respectively as Comma, Colon and Full Stop, and in World War 1 signals stops were signified by AAA. Signals starting with the word CLEAR were an instruction to sender to use ordinary wording instead of a code. Constantly re-occurring letter groups are WEF (for With Effect From), and ACK meaning receipt to be acknowledged).

Aircraft nomenclature

Official publications unfortunately are not consistent in referring to aircraft, and a number of anomalies occur which tend to give the impression that aircraft nomenclature was a haphazard business. The basic concept of the British system of naming and designating aircraft types and their variants is briefly reviewed.

Airship designations

While early British airships had names, the majority of airships under Admiralty control during World War 1 had individual numbers in separate series denoted by significant prefix letters as follows: **C** Coastal, **NS** North Sea, **R** Rigid, **SS** Submarine Scout, **SSE** SS Experimental, **SSP** SS Patrol, **SR** Semi-rigid, **SST** SS Twin (engined), **SSZ** SS Zero Type.

The majority of German airships were operated by the German Navy which allotted numbers prefixed by **L** for Zeppelins, **SL** and **PL** for Schütte-Lanz and Parseval airships respectively. Zeppelins were given a maker's number from No 1, prefixed by **LZ** (Luftschiff Zeppelin). The 'L' naval numbers are often misquoted for the LZ works numbers which were an entirely different series, eg L1, 2, 3 were LZ 14, 18, 24 respectively.

Royal Aircraft Factory designations

Aircraft designations may appear to have been given haphazardly, but like most official matters, there was a system. Perhaps the most bewildering of aircraft designations are the initial letters bestowed by the Royal

Aircraft Factory on official designs, whose original meanings in some cases had little relevance to subsequent design numbers: **AE** Armed/armoured experimental. **AT** Aerial target. **BE** Originally Blériot Experimental for BE1 but applied generally to tractor biplane designs. **BS** Originally Blériot Scout, applied to single-seat experimental tractor designs. **CE** Coastal Experimental. Two CE1s only built. **FE** Farman Experimental as originally applied, but used to qualify pusher aeroplane designs. **HRE** Hydro (ie seaplane) version of RE, see below. **NE** Night-flying Experimental. **RE** Reconnaissance Experimental. **SE** Originally Santos Experimental, but came to mean Scouting Experimental. **TE** Tatin Experimental with propeller at rear.

The emphasis on Experimental was for political reasons; to reassure the public that the function of the national factory was not going into the province of industry. Successive designs in each series was numbered BE1, BE2, BE3, etc. Variants of each design were qualified BE2a, BE2b, BE2c, etc. It will be found, however, that published references go only to BE2e, but World War 1 records frequently refer to BE2f and BE2g. These designations resulted from a production surplus of BE2c and d fuselages, which when fitted with BE2e wings were designated BE2f and BE2g respectively.

Royal Naval Air Service designations

The RNAS used several different systems for designating aircraft. At first they adopted the commercial way of giving the firm's name and simple description, eg 70 hp Short biplane. The serial number of a prototype often became a type designation, eg Short 184 since the first aircraft of this design was serial-numbered 184, similarly the single and two seater Sopwith 1½ Strutters (a nickname quickly adopted officially) were sometimes classed as Types 9700 and 9400 respectively after early representative machines bearing these serial numbers.

Prototypes were often named by their manufacturer's name and class of aircraft. The Air Department (AD) of the Admiralty grouped aircraft into classes as follows: **N1a** Ships' aeroplanes. **N1b** Single-seat fighting seaplanes. **N1c** Reconnaissance fighter seaplane. **N2a** Light flying boat or floatplane. **N2b** Medium flying boat or floatplane. **N3** Large flying boat. These designations account for such designations as the Short N2b or Fairey N3. They should not be confused with the designations F and PV applied by the RNAS stations Felixstowe and Port Victoria (Isle of Grain) to their respective designs.

General aircraft nomenclature

Following the simple description applied to aircraft prior to World War 1, like Blériot Monoplane, Sopwith three-seat biplane, etc, it became usual to name aircraft by a manufacturer's name and a different name for each of the firm's types, eg Sopwith Pup, Sopwith Camel, Sopwith Dolphin, etc. The Aircraft Manufacturing Company designated types after their designer, Geoffrey de Havilland, DH1, DH2, etc. But in 1918 a standard nomenclature was introduced with names allotted to each new aircraft type; the DH10 design, for example, became officially the Amiens. At this stage mark numbers in Roman numerals were introduced to qualify variants of the basic types. Not until 1947 was there the change to the present

Arabic figures, but in 1942 qualifying role letters (B—bomber, F—fighter, TT—target tug, etc) were introduced. More about this will be found later in Notes on notation.

Aircraft were built to meet specifications which were issued by the Air Ministry to the aircraft industry from 1918 onwards, and in some cases these conditioned prototype nomenclature. The Spitfire was first known as the Supermarine F37/34, ie Supermarine's tender to the Air Ministry's Fighter(F) specification No 37 issued in 1934.

Writing on aeronautics

Delving in records and finding new facts, perhaps hitherto unpublished, encourages some enthusiasts to put pen to paper to tell others of their discovery or, having developed an interest, to document the details for the benefit of others. Whether or not the work materialises in print depends on convincing an editor or publisher of its merit. At the present time far too many articles are re-hashes of other works and most tell little more than can be found in standard reference books. New writers may well have something new to tell us all, and editors are perceptive people.

Perhaps the most difficult part of writing is starting. Writers have been known to wrestle for hours on opening lines or paragraphs. But you do not have to start at the beginning. Writing a book or article is not like writing an essay at school or in an examination. You collect facts and figures and you write up the subject in draft. You cannot expect a good rounded presentation of your subject at the first attempt. Re-drafting, re-checking and often re-arranging paragraphs is involved. If all this appears too much effort then authorship is not for you — unless you're a genius and can write without revision.

Team projects may bring more expertise to a report, but team writing may prove impractical unless you have an editor whose decisions all accept. Writing partnerships can lead to difficulties and even co-opting help, most necessary at times, has to be done judiciously. You may be accused of picking the brains of others. The writer had the experience of an enthusiast begging to be allowed to help with a book. To encourage him he was given a small list of aircraft details and asked to re-arrange them in numerical sequence of serial numbers for an appendix. He wanted payment in advance, took several months to do a 20-minute job, submitted a rough draft and, in spite of not having been asked to contribute one word of his own, exclaimed how excited his wife was that his name was going to appear on a book!

The best partnerships are those of author and artist where the respective spheres are clearly defined, or where there is a clear division of subject matter.

Most publishers today like package deals to cut down their administrative work. Under these arrangements the author supplies photos and artwork with his text, and pays the necessary fees taking this into consideration in his negotiations with the publisher.

Writing books

So you want to write a book. There's nothing to it. Anyone with a normal education can — and have it published provided they are prepared to bear the cost. Even for a limited edition, for family and friends, the cost of typesetting, printing and binding would run into four figures.

But that's not what you had in mind, is it? You want a publishing house to produce a book at their expense and pay you a royalty on sales. Now that is possible, but if the publisher is paying for its production he will dictate the type of book he is going to finance and tell you the form it will take. Publishers produce books they think will sell, which sometimes coincides with books authors want to write. You may be lucky with the chance submission of a manuscript, but many books, and particularly aeronautical books, are produced to meet demands.

The old saying that nothing succeeds like success is very true of authorship. Your best recommendation for the acceptance of a book manuscript is an earlier work that sold well. This does mean that the first book is the most difficult hurdle to clear. Most aeronautical authors have worked up to it by steps, progressing from writing articles in limited circulation papers to national aeronautical magazines.

Writing articles

Whatever you write, acceptance of your manuscript for a magazine is subject to the editor's approval. His word is law — and so it should be for he is legally responsible for what is published. As to which editor; there are well over a dozen aviation magazines appearing each month. Send your manuscript to The Editor at the address of the editorial offices given inside the magazine. Do not confuse this with the printer's address, included by law, often at the end of publication.

The easier the manuscript reads to an editor, the better your chances of getting acceptance. Your submission, if accepted, will be the printer's guide so make sure it is submitted properly on good grade, unfolded, A4 size paper, typed double spacing with ample margins for the editor to use for correcting and instructions to the printer. Use one side of the paper only and number the sheets. If you cannot type, you can usually get this done at agencies. It is advisable first to get an estimate and, if accepted, give clear instructions on setting out the work.

The best check before submission is a second reader. Ask a friend or relative to read the papers through, for we are often blind to our own mistakes or foibles. It is also helpful to read a manuscript aloud to hear if it reads well — better still, tape it if you can and listen. The essence of good writing is the maximum of information in the minimum of words consistent with good sense.

Writing for money

Very few writers make a living from writing on aeronautical matters. The majority are part-time contributors. The rewards generally are not high. For magazine articles publishers pay upwards of £10 per thousand words or upward of £5 per page filled with text and/or photos. This depends greatly on the magazine concerned, some paying well below recognised rates. Payment is normally made in arrears, a month after publication.

For books, authors may be paid a lump sum or receive a royalty. The lump sum may be around £250 upwards. A royalty is round about ten per cent of the published price. A publisher would not normally consider a book financially viable unless it would sell some 5,000 copies in three years. So that in the case of a book selling at £5 the author might expect to make $5,000 \times £5 \times 10 \div 100 = £2,500$. Actually it would be less, for royalties are not normally paid on complimentary, review and publicity copies, while royalties on books sold at special discount, eg abroad, are normally smaller. The 'net' is usually closer to eight per cent, in fact — ie £2,000 in the above example. The author, according to the terms of the contract, may be responsible for paying photo reproduction or artist's fees. If the book shows little signs of selling out in a reasonable time the publisher may consider 'remaindering' the book — selling at a lower price for which the royalty will be proportionally lower. On the other hand the book may sell out, a reprint be put in hand and the writer quickly double his money. As remarked earlier, nothing succeeds like success.

Periods of royalty payments, based on sales, are normally at least once a year, and are matters for agreement with the publisher when contracts are drawn up. Some publishers may give advances on signing contract, submission of manuscript or publication — or on all three; again this is a matter for contract between author and publisher. But whether advances or payments on sales or work done, there is another inevitable consideration — tax.

Taxing your writing

Once financial reward ensues from your writing for money you will be well advised to buy a ledger, with your first entry 'This book — 50p' (or whatever it cost). Then think of all the legitimate expenses you have incurred up to that point in pens, paper and perhaps postages and travelling expenses in seeking out relevant information. Log all these expenses down by date in the account book and keep supporting letters on file. Every subsequent expenditure directly attributable to the work — telephone calls, postages, fares, etc, should be logged. In another column put all the money received from publishers.

The point of all this book-keeping is that if you are successful and royalties result, or regular payments for articles ensue, HM Inspector of Taxes will regard this as income and thereby taxable. Under Section 20 of the Finance Act 1956 publishers are bound to notify the Inspector of Taxes, so do not think that your earnings will be overlooked. Normally this tax will be under Schedule D administered by your local tax office, but your income or normal salary from your place of work will be taken into account for the assessment. You are, however, entitled to set legitimate expenses against the total amount received each year. This means closing the books at April 5 each financial year, totalling income and expenses, and subtracting one from the other to determine your profit. Declare your profit to your local tax office with a summary of income and expenses to show how you arrived at your figure. The proportion of tax payable each year will, of course, depend on the annual Budget.

Copyright

The Law of Copyright is often represented as a complicated law, but the principles are simple. Copyright in law is treated as property. You can sell it outright for payment, as is the case with most magazine articles, or give permission in writing, called licence, for a publisher to use your work for which you are paid an agreed royalty on the understanding that he has been given exclusive rights to your work.

Of anything you write, except as an employee, the copyright is yours from the moment it leaves your pen. You cannot copyright facts, alphabetical or numerical sequences, but the general sequence of the words you use, the *way* you relate the facts, are your copyright. You can use any facts you like from other people's books provided you write these facts up in your own way. Quotations are a different matter. But the Law of Copyright is infringed when the 'whole or substantial part thereof' is copied. The 'All Rights Reserved' statement currently appearing in books is not a statement of law. Small quotations from various authors may be essential for a serious study and then it is usual to quote sources as a courtesy. For quotations of any length, permission must be obtained through the publishers and notification given that it is published through their courtesy or in a manner that they may stipulate.

Copyright exists for 50 years from the death of the originator so that for all practical purposes there is copyright existing on all works of aviation; for official publications copyright exists for 50 years from the date of publication.

Pitfalls in writing

There are many pitfalls in writing and much erroneous material has been published. Do not accept the printed word without some reservations; authors make slips and so do printers. Cross-check facts and figures where possible with a second source.

Victory scores are often attributed to pilots and the word ace is freely used. There is no official recognition of an 'ace' and combat reports will reveal the anomalies that occur in giving a tally of scores to pilots. Firstly there is the claim, which may or may not be confirmed, and if confirmed — what as? World War 1 combat reports were assessed under three categories; destroyed, driven down out of control (OOC) and driven down. Scores quoted in books rarely qualify these factors. In World War 2 there are the credits for probables and damaged which, by subsequent reference to German records, may have proved to be aircraft destroyed. Then there are the claims for aircraft destroyed in ground attacks — are these to be treated in the same category as aircraft shot down? Writers need to be most circumspect when quoting scores, particularly comparative scores.

One of the greatest controversies is who shot down von Richthofen; yet some writers, in the face of much evidence to the contrary, blithely state it was Roy Brown. It can only be said that Brown, who made no direct claim to this, was officially *credited* with shooting down this famous German airman.

Beware too, of impugning the character of a gallant man. How could the writer who put 'his victim was of lesser calibre and was shot down in the first burst of fire' be certain that the pilot had less potential than others of his compatriots? Never pass judgement unless you know all the facts.

Make sure that credit is given to the right person in the right way. Second Lieutenant G. R. McCubbin is often credited with shooting down the famous German airman Max Immelmann; certainly he played an important part as the pilot of the aircraft concerned. But aircraft are shot down by guns, not aircraft, and only the observer, Corporal J. H. Waller, had a gun.

The pitfalls of writing on World War 1 are many and some errors are constantly recurring. All German bombers raiding Britain were not Gothas and not all German airships were Zeppelins. Guns were synchronised to fire through the propeller arc — not through the propeller! It is not correct to say that all Camels were built by Sopwith or that Blenheims were all built by Bristol, for the majority were not. In the case of the Hawker Hector, complete production was by Westland. From 1915 onwards there has been extensive sub-contracting throughout the British aircraft industry and the designing firm is not always the manufacturer.

Alexander Pope said that a little learning was a dangerous thing. This can be true of aeronautical writing. Let us take four simple statements:

Blériot was the first man to cross the Channel by air.

Alcock and Brown were the first men to cross the Atlantic by air.

Leefe Robinson destroyed a Zeppelin.

Auxiliary Air Force squadrons fought in the Battle of Britain.

Well, did you know that? It is hoped not, for all four statements are incorrect. Blériot was *not* the first to cross the Channel by air — others had done it a hundred years earlier — by balloon. Alcock and Brown were not the first to fly the Atlantic — an American flying boat preceded them in crossing by air, staging in the Azores; they were the first to do so non-stop. Leefe Robinson destroyed a Shutte-Lanz airship — not a Zeppelin one. The Auxiliary Air Force did not serve as such in World War 2 at all, for the day war was declared the Auxiliary Air Force was embodied in the RAF and the former AAF squadrons became RAF squadrons. The City and County titles were retained, and for a time they were manned by AAF personnel, but as casualties took their toll so permanent RAF or Volunteer Reserve aircrew took over in the absence of any AAF entry during the war.

We rarely see our faults as others see them. Our mistakes, repetitions and ponderous statements are not realised — until enlightenment comes and that is usually when the manuscript is already at press and it's much too late to alter. But don't be downhearted. It happens to us all. And perhaps you'll do better next time!

Notes on notation

When it comes to serious writing for publication, notation can be a problem. How do you put dates — '5th January 1945' or 'Jan 5, 1945, or some other way? Do you write 'RAF' or 'R.A.F.'? These are matters that will depend on the publisher's house style. Some publishers issue a guide to authors and for those that do not an obvious guide is a previous published work by that particular publisher.

Styles vary, but where possible take the correct, simplest and most commonly used way. The modern style is to do away with stops where possible — 'USAF' not 'U.S.A.F.' and 'No 1' not 'No. 1'. Since this saves time writing, typing and type-setting, and makes not one bit of difference in meaning, it is a trend to be encouraged.

Aircraft serial numbers appear written in different forms — 'K 5054' or

'K.5054', but there is only one correct way — K5054 — the way it appeared on the aircraft.

British service aircraft mark numbers should be written in the form appropriate to the period; see General aircraft nomenclature referred to earlier. Thus, the form would vary as follows: pre-1942 — Tiger Moth II; 1942-1947 — Tiger Moth TII; post-1947 — Tiger Moth T2.

Aircraft names should be in normal style, thus Spitfire, not in quotes 'Spitfire' or italics *Spitfire* which should be used for aircraft individual names as apart from type names, eg the Liberator *Lady Luck.*

German designation should be in the form Do 17, Ju 87, etc, without stops but FW 190 or BV 222. This is because, eg Do is an abbreviation of **Do**rnier and FW an abbreviation of **F**ocke **W**ulf. This leads us to the controversial Bf 109 or Me 109. Bf is correct for 108, 109 and 110, the designs of Bayerische Flugzeugwerke and is so used in German records, but it is in order to say 'the pilot reported Me 109s' since Me 109 was the term by which they were invariably known during World War 2 to the British.

Russian designations are similarly Po-2 or Tu-124, being abbreviations of design bureaux named after famous designers — **Po**likarpov and **Tu**polev. An anomaly is MiG (written this way) because it refers to the joint efforts of **Mi**koyan and **G**urevich. Three letters are used for the single name in the case of **Yak**olev.

With American aircraft designations, a hyphen between the role letters and numbers is an essential part of the designation, eg B-17, P-51.

Unfortunately official histories are not good guides to correct notation, but the editors of the aeronautical monthlies, weeklies and the fortnightly are experienced aeronautical journalists and can soon knock a manuscript into trim. Some publishers may well assume that you, as the author, use correct notation and the responsibility is then squarely upon your shoulders.

Researching aerial warfare over Britain

With all the books that have been written about the aerial activities over the United Kingdom during World War 2, only a small fraction of the events have ever been detailed. Even with the privately published backgrounds to the various digs at crash sites that have taken place, only a fraction of the air activity of World War 2 has been thoroughly researched. In the first place aerial activity was very widespread and news at the time was suppressed in the interests of security; secondly, many of the references in books have been culled from earlier books and are thereby repetitive about particular incidents. The publication in 1972 of a *Lincolnshire Air War 1939-1945,* by S. Finn, detailing the crashes and other aircraft incidents in and over Lincolnshire, gave an insight into the research that could be done in an area survey and its author, I feel sure, would be the first to admit that this book, detailed as it is, is not exhaustive. Whether you live in Lincolnshire, or elsewhere in the United Kingdom, there is much to be researched. The reader may well know that there was intense activity during the Battle of Britain and the Blitz in the winter of 1940/41, and that in 1944 there were the V-weapon attacks. But practically every night there was activity of some sort, and it has largely gone unrecorded.

To prove the point, one mid-war night is taken at random and summarised — the night of April 9/10 1941. Not a very significant date, but both RAF and Luftwaffe were active.

RAF Bomber Command that night made 99 sorties. There was an attack on industrial plants at Berlin by 36 Wellingtons, 24 Hampdens, 17 Whitleys and three Stirlings. Bombs were dropped on Templehof Aerodrome among other targets. Eight Wellingtons and a single Manchester set out to bomb the Bremer Vulcan naval shipyards at Vegesack, while seven Wellingtons attacked Emden and three Hampdens dropped mines in the Frisian Islands area. Eight of the 99 aircraft were lost and two Wellingtons reported encounters with Me 110s and a Hampden gunner claimed an Me 109 destroyed.

Fighter Command intruders were out, eight aircraft operating separately; airfields at Bethune, Caen, Caprycke, Evreux, Freux, Lille and Merville being claimed as bombed, a goods train was machine-gunned and a direct hit made on a railway to the south of Rouen. A Coastal Command Beaufort made a night torpedo attack on a merchant ship and Hudsons bombed an aluminium works and dropped leaflets over Norway.

That night the Luftwaffe concentrated on Birmingham, bombs starting to fall at 21.35 hours in the Bordesley Green area, followed by incendiary attacks over the northern and eastern districts, then spreading over Aston, King's Heath, Small Heath and Stetchford districts. Fire brigades were out dealing with fires at works — Austin's at Northfield, BSA at Small Heath, Birmingham Electric Furnaces and Dunlop at Erdington, Wolseley Motors at Ward End, Lewis's, Perfection Steel Tubes at Aston and Parkingson's Stove Company at Stetchford. Snow Hill station was hit and so were lines near New Street, and Newton Street Police Station had a direct hit.

Two hours later another attack developed in the Tynemouth area, flares dropping at 23.24 hours heralding the attack. There were soon serious fires burning at Sunderland including Brown's Store and Steel's Warehouse. Several smaller fires were reported at Whitley Bay, two shops were destroyed and a canteen set on fire at Swan Hunter's Wallsend shipyard, works were damaged at Jarrow, timber yards set alight at South Shields and the X-Ray department of the Preston Institution at Tynemouth was demolished.

That same night, over a dozen airfields were attacked over a wide area — Linton, Lindholme and Leeming in Yorkshire, Scampton in Lincolnshire, Bourn and Steeple Morden in Cambridgeshire, Cottesmore in Rutland, Cranfield in Bedfordshire, Middle Wallop in Hampshire where a hangar was damaged, Colerne in Wiltshire where the single attacker swooped down to 200 feet, West Raynham in Norfolk where No 4 hangar roof was damaged and two aircraft inside, Hampstead Norris in Berkshire where the enemy aircraft followed one of our own aircraft coming in to land as did the attacker of Wittering in Northamptonshire.

Beaufighters shot an He 111 down near Ringwood, another enemy aircraft 12 miles north-west of Wittering and damaged a Ju 88 over Middle Wallop. Two Hurricanes attacked and destroyed a Ju 88 off Lowestoft for the loss of one Hurricane. A Defiant destroyed an enemy aircraft near Bramcote and others exchanged fire over the Biggin Hill and Kirton-in-Lindsey areas. A Havoc off Portland sighted and attacked another of the enemy. Altogether five He 111s and two Ju 88s were destroyed by aircraft and AA guns claimed another aircraft.

The foregoing is a mere sketchy brief of the main aerial activities over Britain in one night of the war that lasted five years. This night's activities alone could be expanded into several books if researched in detail. The field is wide open. There is much new ground to be covered by general studies in depth over limited periods, or an overall air war study for a limited area, such as a county in the case of northern areas and small counties, and in the vicinity of towns or airfields in the case of places like Eastbourne or Coltishall.

Collecting facts and figures to record air history is the least expensive pursuit in aeronautica. In these days when many villages have their own privately run newsletters, your own contribution to parish history could be on well-researched aeronautical aspects. There is much to be delved into.

AIRCRAFT PHOTOGRAPHY

Most air enthusiasts treasure photographs of aircraft or aerial activities in some form, prints from an original negative, copy prints or reproductions in publications. As far as aviation is concerned, the quality of early photographs, taken on large glass plate negatives, is likely to be as good, if not better, than many photographs taken today. On the other hand, prints of 50 or 60 years ago are liable to turn brown (some were printed in sepia) and fade over the years. At the first hint of this, the pictures should be re-copied by a reliable photographer before too much detail is lost. Old sepia prints copy particularly well.

With photographs, a print from the original negative is preferable to a copy of a print which involves making a new negative, a 'copy neg'. With each successive copying a picture is slightly degraded. It is difficult to tell a picture several times removed from the original, from a poor initial photograph. On the other hand it is usually easy to tell if a print was produced from a copy negative of a photo in a published work, as under a magnifying glass the 'screen' (series of dots making up the picture) will become evident which is absent from direct photography.

Never use a hard lead pencil or ball-point pen when marking information or numbering on the back of photographic prints. These can make an indentation and mark the surface of the picture. A felt-tipped pen is best, but on some thin paper this may show through. If in doubt mark at the top or bottom, corresponding to sky or ground areas, or write on paper and stick to this on the back of the print. Similarly, if using a rubber stamp, be careful not to over-ink as the liquid might be absorbed by the paper and spoil the image. When marking up a print for an enlargement of a part, perhaps to show a marking or emblem, the best way is to overlay the print with transparent paper, tracing paper will do, and mark this up. To hold the transparent paper in place, have it an inch deeper than the photo, fold this extra piece back level with the top of the photo and secure it to the back with Cow gum. Tape can be used but it has to be very carefully removed, to avoid it taking up some of the backing, unless you use masking tape.

Prints are best stored in boxes, the printing paper boxes are just the right sizes and provide the essentials of keeping prints flat and out of strong light. To avoid scratching, soft paper between prints is desirable. Negatives are much more delicate and should be stored separated one from the other. Transparent envelopes are ideal as they provide a separating surface and permit the subject matter to be seen when held to the light without extracting the negative. They too, should be kept flat. Old films in reels, where there has been direct contact, now present great difficulties if the subject matter is to be preserved. Flexibility is lost after the passage of years and attempts to run the reels can result in a complete breaking up of the film. To re-constitute the films often means copying every frame. Stills from old films is one new source for adding to historical collections.

Official photographic records

For record purposes, most air forces of the world have photographic records for various reasons. In the RAF these were classified in 1937 by letters used in RAF photo references ledgers as follows: **A** Operations and Intelligence. **B** Training (particularly photographic training). **C** Co-operation with Royal Navy and Army. **D** Requests from other Government Departments. **E** To illustrate official reports. **F** Publicity and press.

With the exception of photographs taken by official photographers for publicity and record purposes, which were passed to the Imperial War Museum for custody, the bulk have been destroyed. Millions of photos have been taken, particularly aerial views; it was not unusual in 1918 for over a thousand photos to be taken in one day on one Front. Fortunately, thousands of photos of all types taken over the past 60 years, which have officially been destroyed, have actually been acquired by individuals and have found their way into collections. Many in more recent years have been donated to the Imperial War Museum and the RAF Museum.

Official photo markings

Those holding or perusing the old official photographs are often hampered by the fact that the official registers of photographs compiled by units have rarely survived and the clue to the subject lies in the significance of the cryptic markings at the base or at the corners of these photos. To give an example: **A55: DA: 892 14.1.18.** This would mean that it was the 892nd photo taken by A Flight, No 55 Squadron of the 41st Wing (fourth and first letters of the alphabet), dated January 14 1918, a day the official communiqué will show that the squadron took 52 photos of a raid on Karlsruhe. Up to 26 a Wing might be represented two ways, eg the 18th Wing as AH (first and eighth letters) or just as R (18th letter of the alphabet). Where units other than squadrons were concerned, a significant letter or letters were used, eg CFS for Central Flying School.

Early in the 1920s, the RAF decreed a comprehensive four-line system for negative marking, either by scratching the emulsion or scraping a portion of the emulsion away and applying a marking ink. These markings would, of course, reproduce on all prints so that its origin and details would appear. A typical marking would be in the form:

28C105
30F695368
21.5.23 09.50
F = 22″

Line 1 gave the unit number (28 Squadron), the series number (C) and the individual number in that series. It was advised that when 999 was reached a new series should appertain from No 1. *Line 2* gave the Map Sheet and position reference, or subject as appropriate. *Line 3* gave date and time. *Line 4* gave focal length of lens.

Towards the end of 1926 it was decided that a classifying suffix should be placed after the photo number in the first line as follows: **FV** For film

Right *View taken from an unattributed postcard with brief caption '38-LONDON CROYDON AIR PORT'. Lufthansa Ju52/3m, named Rudolf Berthold after the famous World War 1 airman, seen here by the terminal buildings which can still be seen today in the middle of an industrial complex, not far from Waddon Station where a pub is still called 'The Propeller'.*

Right *Background to many World War 1 photos and the early days of aviation, the Brooklands motor racing track, which can still be traced round. Martinsyde Elephant seen circa 1916 (Martinsyde).*

Below *This replica of the Billing B9 biplane took some 400 man-hours to restore by a group of airmen serving at RAF Gatow, Berlin, and flew in the film 'Those Magnificent Men in their Flying Machines' (CPRO RAF Germany).*

Above *The intricate woodwork of the inside of a World War 1 hangar has to be seen to be appreciated — and you can appreciate it at the RAF Museum which incorporated such a hangar at Hendon, seen here before the museum opened* (RAF Museum).

Left *Duxford barrack blocks north of the airfield in the pseudo-Georgian style of the RAF expansion period of the mid-1930s* (K. M. Robertson collection).

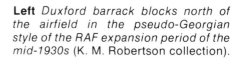

Left *Duxford airfield architecture seen during World War 2. Looking west from the guardroom on left, 1917-style hangars; middle the admin block built in the style of the 1930s; married quarters to the right built in the 1920s and Nissen huts beyond erected 1939-41* (K. M. Robertson collection).

Right *Typical of the aeronautical monuments that are to be found. The inscription reads: 'The first aeroplane flight in Great Britain was made from this hillock by S. F. Cody on the morning of 16th October 1908. He took off in a westerly direction and flew for a distance of 1390 feet. This model was made in the workshops of the Royal Aircraft Establishment and presented by the Society of British Aerospace Companies to the Royal Air Force Officer's Mess, Farnborough, on the 6th September 1964'* (RAE 168459).

Below *Classical association. The plaque between the door and window in this house at Bath that Jane Austen lived here — the board relates to the Chief Instructor's office of No 7 (Observers) School of Aeronautics, Bath.*

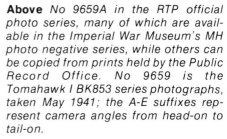

Above *No 9659A in the RTP official photo series, many of which are available in the Imperial War Museum's MH photo negative series, while others can be copied from prints held by the Public Record Office. No 9659 is the Tomahawk I BK853 series photographs, taken May 1941; the A-E suffixes represent camera angles from head-on to tail-on.*

Above left *Negative No PPG4315 is RAF number of the Austrian Berg fighter and the official stamp it bears states that this number should be quoted if further copies are required — but, alas, it is a forgotten series.*

Left *In the immediate post-war years the Air Technical Publications periodical Air Review contained many interesting photos of the period. Only a few negatives of this collection, which ran to over 1,000, are extant. This print, ATP669 of the series, shows the Miles M28 Mercury 4 later G-AGVX, HB-EED, VH-AKH and VH-AKC.*

Left *The Real Photographs series runs into thousands. Here, No 444 in the series (the negative number usually appeared in this way at either bottom left or right) shows the DH14A with Napier Lion engine (RP444).*

Above *Example of the interesting aeronautical subjects on pre-war postcards, a BE1 undergoing a field engine change circa 1912. From the F. Scovell & Co 'Expert Military and Commercial Photographs' series.*

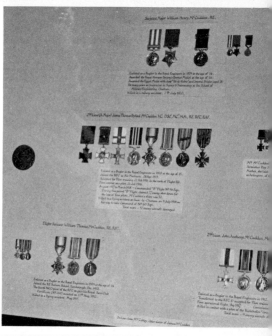

Right *Perhaps the most famous 'clutch' of air medals ever displayed. At the centre, the medals of James Thomas Byford McCudden, VC, DSO, MC, MM; at the top those of his father Sergeant Major W. H. McCudden RE, and below those of his two brothers, Flight Sergeant W. T. and 2nd Lieutenant J. A. McCudden, both of whom were killed flying in the RFC.*

Right *Several collections of photographs have been marketed over the years for book illustrations, purporting to be genuine World War 1 action shots taken with a wire-operated, strut-mounted camera. If you can conceive that a pilot could manoeuvre his aircraft to take just the right angle of an aerial collision, then you may accept such shots as genuine.*

Unser erfolgreicher Kampfflieger
Leutnant Röth

ADOLPHE PÉGOUD
Sergent-Aviateur

Above *Many of Germany's famous air-men of World War 1 were featured on Postkartenvertrieb W. Sanke of Berlin. This is No 647 of this famous Postcard series.*

Below *The 'den' of a 'buff'. The negative files and records of William T. Larkins, 1956.*

Above *The French had this CP1 series of postcards of famous airmen. Shown is No 160 featuring 'Adolphe Pegoud Sergent-Aviateur'.*

Below *No 47 in the Aerofilms series of postcards sold at Air Displays in the 1930s.*

SIR ALAN COBHAM'S AIR DISPLAY

THE HANDLEY PAGE 'CLIVE' 22 PASSENGER AIR LINER

Joseph Simpson was the first to put on canvas the multi-coloured lozenge-patterned dyed fabric used by the Germans. To have presented this view of a Hannover two-seater in such detail means that he had studied in detail a captured example (IWM Q67115).

Above 'Books are the very fuel of aeronautica'. As part of the RAF 50th Anniversary Celebrations, an exhibition of flying books was held in London. Here, in a lively discussion of the tomes is, left to right, Sir Barnes Wallis, G. R. Duval, AFM author of a book in the famous Putnam series and of ten books on the Bradford Barton aircraft pictorial surveys, Bruce Robertson and the late D. A. Russell, who launched and maintained a consistent styling of Harleyford books for over 20 years.

Below The most popular of hobbies among air enthusiasts — modelling. These Airfix models presented to two of the most famous World War 2 fighter pilots, General Galland (left) and Wing Commander R. R. Stanford Tuck DSO, DFC, were in the markings of the aircraft they flew at some period of the war.

taken vertically. **FP** For film taken obliquely. **G** For ground photographs. **P** For oblique (Panoramic) photography. **V** For vertical air-to-ground shots.

In addition to the focal length, the height above sea level (later changed to height above ground level) was marked on line four after the focal length. At the side of the photograph arrows might refer to pinpoints or co-ordinates, and on each photo an arrow indicated north.

During World War 2 further qualifying initials appeared: **M** — Mirror, **MF** — Moving Film, **NT** — Night Photograph (ie taken with flash-bomb). **RX** — Infra-red photography and **TOPO,** short for topographical, for pictures taken for survey purposes. From 1942, the great increase in reconnaissance photography led to blocks of series numbers allotted to camera positions as follows: Oblique — from 0001; Port wing — from 1001; Starboard wing — from 2001; Port rear — from 3001; Starboard rear — from 4001; Vertical rear — from 5001; Additional rear — from 6001; Vertical front or in wing — from 7001; and Additional front — from 8001.

Official photo series

Millions of the prints taken have little value, but thousands were of historical significance. One of the most valuable series cannot now be traced. This was the RAF London Photo Centre set up during the closing stages of World War 1 to record RAF activities. Beautiful sepia whole plate prints were run off for the press on a wide variety of RAF activities, including an aerial survey of biblical lands, aircraft and mechanical transport. The Centre also used RAF station photography as general agents, eg the Felixstowe Seaplane Base photo section were tasked with recording the surrender of the German U-boats. At their Centre, Goschen Buildings, 12-13 Henrietta Street, Covent Garden, London WC2, they gave film displays to the public on such intriguing subjects as 'Alighting Trials on HMS *Furious*'; 'Tails Up — Scenes of Life of an RAF pilot in France'; 'A Tour round an Airship Station'; 'Launching the Porte Flying Boat', etc.

Perhaps the most valued series of all, of which examples are avidly sought by collectors, are the RTP (Research & Technical Publications) Photographic Section series which started in the 1920s and carried through under the Air Ministry, later the Ministry of Aircraft Production and then the Ministry of Supply to post-World War 2 days. This series mainly concerned ground views of all new or specially equipped aircraft at makers, testing or experimental establishments. By 1944 the series had reached No 12500, and each number was of a different subject. Normally five different views were taken of each aircraft, reflected in suffix letters to the number, usually as follows: **A** Head-on view; **B** ¾ front view; **C** Profile view; **D** ¾ rear view; and **E** View from rear.

These pictures were rarely released to the press as many were then classed as secret and a common marking on the back was OUO (Official Use Only). Post-war many of the photos in this series were made available to the Imperial War Museum in their MH series and can be ordered by their allotted MH number. During the 1960s a large number of these photos were offered for sale by a bookshop and were acquired by collectors.

The main series of official photographs have qualifying prefix letters, those including aircraft subjects being: **A** Admiralty series World War 2 and subsequently. **AM** Air Ministry from 1920. **C** Imperial War Museum, World War 2, mainly taken from the air. **CAN** Imperial War Museum, World War 2, taken in Canada. **CF** and **CFP** Imperial War Museum, World War 2, Far East. **CH** Imperial War Museum, World War 2, general European series. **CHR** Imperial War Museum, World War 2, Rhodesia. **CI** Imperial War Museum, World War 2, India. **CL** Imperial War Museum, World War 2 'Liberation series' starting June 6 1944. **CM** Imperial War Museum, World War 2, Middle East (also CMP series). **CNA** Imperial War Museum, World War 2, North Africa. **D** Ministry of Defence, post-World War 2, Display Records. **E** Imperial War Museum and Australian War Memorial collection of World War 1 Australian Flying Corps pictures. **H** Ministry of Defence, mainly 1919-1939 private copyright. **HU** Imperial War Museum, private copyright. **MH** Imperial War Museum, mainly experimental and prototype aircraft of Martlesham Heath collection. **PA** Public Archives of Canada. **PL** Canadian Forces Photos. **PRB** Air Ministry, later Ministry of Defence, post-World War 2 RAF publicity pictures (all black and white). **Q** Imperial War Museum, World War 1. **R** Air Ministry post-World War 2 to February 1950, Central Office of Information subsequently. **RE** Archives of Canada. **RUS** Imperial War Museum, World War 2, RAF in Russia. **T** and **TN** Ministry of Defence, recent years. RAF publicity pictures. Colour series.

In recent years the Ministry of Defence has ceased supplying prints to purchasers from the general public, of their PRB, T and TN series and limits sales to the Press for publication. The H series can be perused for research purposes by application to the Ministry of Defence (AHB), Lacon House, Theobalds Road, London, WC1X 8RY. RAF station photographers have taken photographs over the past 60 years but no central record exists and negatives in general have been destroyed as ephemeral interest matter.

Some of these series cover general military subjects with aeronautical aspects included. Also, some pictures are anachronisms; for example a World War 2 personality may have a 'flashback' World War 1 picture included in a World War 2 series. The Photographic Library at the IWM can be visited by prior appointment with the Keeper of Photographs.

Gaps in the records

Unhappily many of the photographic records of World War 1 have been lost. Much of Germany's aeronautical archives were destroyed during World War 2 in the bombing of Berlin. The Regia Aeronautica's records in Rome were plundered by troops as spoils of war; one serviceman brought a suitcase full of Italian aircraft photos to Britain to sell to a British aeronautical magazine. The writer knows of one magazine that refused the offer, but it is still not known publicly where these records ended up.

The original glass negatives recording the history of the RAF taken by the RFC and later RAF School of Photography, Farnborough, were smashed and disposed of as broken glass, at the very time efforts were being made for their preservation and cataloguing. In 1957 the United States Air Force completed the destruction of 44,000 original 8 × 10-inch negatives of World War 1, the 1920s and early 1930s. While it was true the negatives were deteriorating and the Force had the good sense to have them micro-filmed, a reproduction from the small current negative is a poor substitute for a direct reproduction from a whole plate negative.

Manufacturers' photographic records have suffered over the years by the contraction of the aviation industry and the integration into the two large groups, British Aircraft Corporation and the Hawker Siddeley Group, whereby firms like Blackburn, De Havilland, Vickers, etc, have lost their identities. Avro, in particular, have suffered by loss of photos in fires.

On the credit side

On the other hand, some magnificent collections have survived with, in particular, thousands of World War 1 German aircraft photos being acquired by American collectors. The official 'H' series controlled by the Ministry of Defence is a typical example of current awareness of historical records. A senior RAF officer had asked for a photograph of a Hawker Hart and was astonished to be told that no official pictures existed. The Imperial War Museum was concerned mainly with the two World Wars and the photographic records of the RAF between the wars had disappeared. Conscious of this gap in records an Air Ministry Information Officer, C. C. H. Cole, contacted many serving and ex-service RAF personnel to obtain their photographs to fill this gap. Permission was obtained to copy and reproduce as required and so the 'H' collection was built up to some 3,000 prints, including many official prints that had been deteriorating at various units. While the pictures were mainly between the wars, other good representative aircraft and activity shots not available from other sources have been added.

Many photographs appear with reports on Air Matters in the Public Record Office, Kew, and arrangements can be made to have these copies for a fee within a week. Also the Royal Air Force and Fleet Air Arm Museums are constantly adding to their collections from both official and private sources.

Photographs of your own

For those making their own photographic record of aircraft the camera is, of course, the essential component, but it need not be an expensive one. The more complicated a camera, the more are the mistakes that can be made through inaccurate settings, and the results often not nearly so good as by someone using a cheap popular make. But this rather depends on whether you are merely recording aircraft close-up at airfields, or more distant views with telephoto lens and ground-to-air shots.

It need hardly be said that colour will make a far more attractive and revealing collection than black and white, and well worth the extra cost. An adequate camera to record aircraft on the ground in colour can still be purchased for well under £25.

Style and size

A major decision is the form your collection will take — prints or slides. If it is prints, some firms offer cheap developing and printing in an 8 cm (3⅛-inch) size square, but think twice before you decide on your standard. A square format, while suitable for family groups, is unsuitable for aircraft which are mostly long thin subjects. Postcard size has both the right proportions for presenting aircraft and it is a compromise between the too small and too expensive.

Slides in the standard 35 mm size have to be seen properly projected to appreciate the high quality definition that can be achieved with standard film used in a cheap camera. The battery-operated viewers with magnifying glasses should be regarded simply as instruments for a quick check on subject matter. This does involve incurring the expense of a projector and a portable screen, but this may well be a shared cost with the family.

Rather than get a cheap projector and progress to a more expensive one, aim for a good projector in basic form, to which the trimmings such as remote control and rotary magazine can be added later.

For most slides, processing costs are paid when you buy the films, but there are several processing firms sending out Freepost envelopes to get your custom. When you can, buy your film in the winter for the next summer season's air shows. In this way you defeat to some degree the continuing inflationary rises, and the summer seasonal rise when demand is highest, as well as making use of the winter reductions some shops give.

Lest the writer be accused of being sponsored, he will not state his film manufacturers preferences, but he does advise that you try several at first, note the prices paid and results achieved, make due allowance for weather conditions, and come to your own decision.

Ab initio

For the uninitiated the rules of good photography are briefly detailed. Read and follow the working instructions given with your camera. Avoid taking photos into the sun. Before you snap make sure that your fingers and thumbs, and the case flap, are clear of the lens. When you do snap make sure the camera is held rigidly steady — this you can practise with the camera empty; camera movement means blurred photos. Immediately after taking a shot, turn the spool to the next frame number so that your camera is ready for instant use. Put the frame number and the picture details in your notebook — what to put is given below.

Now for the particular points of aeronautical photography. Wherever possible get the identification marking of the aircraft, civil registration or military serial number in the picture. There are thousands of photos of some aircraft types, but perhaps only a few are of the particular one you photographed. From its identity, its history can be traced. Avoid where possible cutting off wingtips and tail. As for the best angle, sun and conditions permitting, imagine that you are going to make a model of the aircraft and want a photo guide for the markings — that's the best angle.

Recording your collection

The essential information required with aircraft photographs is: type, identity, date and place. Type need not be established right away if you are not very expert at identification; the identity markings should establish this. If the identity marking (civil registration or military serial) is not visible note other details, with time and place, for each frame. This is not only for your personal records and interest, but these are the details people who may buy copies from you, or exchange with you, will want to know.

If you want to trade photos, you may be surprised to find that pictures you consider gems may not be regarded as such by others. The Shuttleworth Collection of veteran and vintage aircraft, and the Spitfires and Hurricanes of the RAF's Battle of Britain Flight, may seen very attractive subjects to you. For your own collection they are essentials, but do not expect these to be saleable items, for everyone photographs them.

Displaying your collection

To display your collection, the system of a hundred years has no equal — the album. If you wish to group aircraft by types or manufacturer, then a loose-leaf album is essential. The album will keep the photos flat and away from direct light, both most necessary for long term preservation. Do not stick down but use transparent corner attachments, or modern transparent cover albums, so that photos can be easily re-arranged if required.

Photographs that you take yourself, provided that you are not being employed to take them, are your copyright. If you trade or sell prints the purchaser should only reproduce them with your permission, unless you wish to sell the copyright. But only a fraction of the photos taken have any value for reproduction. Current aircraft photography in aviation magazines comes mainly from staff photographers and publicity photos sent free to the editors from the Services and industry. A number of enthusiasts also advertise their pictures in aeronautical magazines for sale to enthusiasts. Most of these are photographers who started their collections as hobbies. To be successful you must have a good range to offer, good photography, unusual subjects and money to advertise your wares.

Cataloguing your collection

Whether your collection remains private or becomes commercial, some system of identification is necessary. You will need a register to put down the essential details already referred to, so you will need to number your negatives as your collection grows. Some collectors break their registering down into series by nationalities and manufacturers, with qualifying or significant prefix letters. This causes complications, for you are unable to foresee the register space you should allot to each series, and mergers of companies complicate the issue — and how do you classify a French aircraft in British service? It is much simpler to number and register all your negatives in a straightforward numbering system from No 1, and have a simple card index in alphabetical sequence giving types, airlines, etc with reference to a photo number in your register.

By all means have your personal identifying prefix letter to the whole series, perhaps your initials, and then an uncomplicated single numerical series. It is advisable to stamp prints on the back, with your notice of copyright and reference number. A simple toy shop printing set is adequate for this purpose in the form —

John A Smith Photograph
Copyright 1983
Reference No JAS/*186*

The copyright starts from the date you took the photograph and lasts for 50* years, and to save changing the stamp for each numbered print, the register number, shown in italics, can be put in with a soft pen. Never write with a ball pen as this may leave its mark on the print surface. Do not over-ink your stamp and make sure the print is dry before you place another with it.

*The law, as amended 1956, gives 50 years from date of first publication.

COLLECTORS' ITEMS

Aeronautical books

Books are the very fuel of aeronautica; many an enthusiast had his interest first kindled by a particular book; they provide information and illustrations for study, interest or relaxation, and they are both easily accessible and durable. Most air enthusiasts can boast at least a small library and so become collectors of books. For permanent use there is only one sure way of acquiring books, and that is by buying them! It is constantly said that books now are becoming so dear that they are pricing themselves out of the market; of course they are dearer than they were in the past, but it is a rise proportionally less than the rise in incomes. However, the average enthusiast certainly cannot afford all the books that he or she would like, and ways and means are suggested of adding to your bookshelves without a crippling outlay, by buying wisely, taking up offers and reductions and buying second-hand.

First-hand

There are five ways of buying books, but the really good books in your sphere of interest are worth buying the normal way. The normal way is, of course, from a bookshop. But, firstly, how do you know what is available? Advertisements in aeronautical magazines are an obvious source, but then products have been known to fall below the claims of advertisers. Book reviews in aeronautical magazines might give some guide, but the overall standard of reviewing is not high. Publishers often send out a 'blurb' with their review copies which reviewers can quote verbatim and so advertise their product. You can sometimes discern this for yourself when the review corresponds closely to the blurb on the dust jacket of a book. There is another factor; a magazine publisher could be embarrassed with a review that condemns a book by a publishing house supporting his magazine by paying for advertising space. The highest standard of reviewing is usually found in professional magazines, like the Royal Aeronautical Society *Journal*, and in the enthusiasts' publications, like *Air Britain Digest*, with the reservation that some enthusiasts tend to pick on small details. The surest way of all, is to view the book in a library at leisure and then make up your mind.

As to actually buying the book, it is surprising the number of people who think that you have to write to the publishers. Yet they are normal people who appreciate that their morning cornflakes come from a local grocer and not by application to Messrs Kellogg. Books come from bookshops. Your local bookshop should know the drill and welcome your custom.

There is such a vast range of books available that you cannot expect your particular local to stock your particular requirement, but all he needs is title, author and publishing house. He will have the address. Unbelievable as it may seem, some prospective buyers write to the printers. Make sure that the name you give is the *publisher's*, not the *printer's* who are bound to have their name and address displayed as a point of law. On the other hand, some enthusiasts' publications are available only by application to the sales department of the organisation.

For new books there is no need to 'shop around' like a housewife. Due to author/publisher contractual agreements and other conditions of sale, booksellers are in no position to make special cut-price offers or random reductions. But it is possible to buy books at a much reduced price when they are remaindered — the selling out of stock of books that are not selling well. A book being remaindered is not likely to be re-published, so it is something of a last chance. Because a book did not sell may not mean that it is a poor book, but rather that it was too specialised for a wide appeal — but that appeal could be your particular field. One of the best areas for picking up bargains in remaindered books is the Holborn district of London. The Charing Cross Road area has the wider selection of books in general, but some shops there have had remaindered books still listed at full selling price. To give a good bargain example — *Memoirs of the Old Balloonatic,* a 1914-18 War narrative by an RFC kite balloon officer, Goderic Hodges, was published by Kimber's in 1972 at £3.25; it was picked up by the author at a bookshop near Holborn Viaduct for £1.05. This type of book is a good investment, for there are very few books on service ballooning and not many survivors now capable of adding to the range. After remaindering, books will become classed as out of print and thereby unattainable; their price may well rise over the years and the book become a treasured collector's item. The beauty of remaindered books is that they are usually in mint condition, for in no way are they second-hand books, but you take pot luck on what is offered. The books you really want are usually only obtained by buying at full price.

Another way of getting a book cheap is a paperback edition. There is no way of predicting remaindering or paperback publication, but since you cannot possibly have afforded all in the vast range of books on aeronautical subjects, this is one way of adding to your collection the cut-price way. It is the narratives and air novels that chiefly get put into paperback form. A typical example is the famous 1914-18 War classic *Winged Victory*, published by Jonathan Cape in 1934 which became a much sought collector's item until 1969 when Sphere Books published it at 6/- (30p), but it is now (1983) out of print again. The three volumes *Royal Air Force 1939-45,* were republished at £2 per volume, so paperbacks can be expensive, but as Volume 1 is already out of print, any reprinting will cost much more.

Second-hand

Now we come to second-hand books. These can be obtained at three very different types of establishment. The real collector's pieces will be at a much higher price than when published. Books that went out of print many years ago can now only be obtained second-hand. For a particular old book the London specialist shops are some of the best places to try. Beaumont's Aviation Literature specialises in aeronautical books and

W. E. Hersants of Highgate carry a wide range of aeronautical books. In the provinces there is Aero Books — The Bicester Bookshop and Aero Mart of Marlborough Road, Ipswich. These are specialist shops rather than second-hand bookshops for they deal also with current aeronautical books from British and foreign publishers.

Second-hand bookshops in towns around the country are delightful places in which to browse, and many have good bargains in aircraft books. One can usually be found at seaside towns where holiday-makers, with leisure time, make them a viable proposition; the writer picked up a signed copy of Sir Arthur Longmore's *From Sea to Sky* at Folkestone for 30p in 1972. Antique dealers often have a display of books for sale and sometimes a cheap shelf. While central London is the best place for remaindered books, second-hand books will be found to be much cheaper in the suburbs. Hardbacks of the book club type like *The Dam Busters* and *Reach for the Sky* could still be picked up for 10p in Greater London in 1983. Thus the collector could fill a shelf with some of the best of the narratives. Books on naval and military subjects may also have quite an amount of air action, for example, Terence Robertson's *Channel Dash.*

The second-hand furniture and junk shop is yet another source of book supply. These dealers often bid for the contents of old houses that have to be cleared and dispose of it as scrap metal, second-hand furniture and fittings and such books as were left. These dealers are usually not so knowledgeable of the book world as antique dealers, and some very good old books go for a song — sometimes even aircraft photo albums. Often a price is not displayed and the price asked might be according to what the proprietor thinks you would pay. The best ploy for these shopping sorties is old clothes and worn shoes. It often makes the difference between '25p each, Sir' and '10p each, Mate'.

Finally we come to the best bargain counter of all, the jumble sale. Here are books cheaper than anywhere else and by buying them you are probably helping a worthy cause. You must be prepared for the rough and tumble of the initial rush as the ladies make for the clothes counter, brushing all else aside, and to be disappointed in the selection of books — often the leftovers from an earlier sale. But occasionally there are amazing bargains. One of the best London jumble book sales is the annual Colfe's School Summer Fair at Lee. Thousands of books are spread over many tables and are added to throughout the sale to fill up spaces left by those sold. However, one of the boys may well read this and get the price put up on aircraft books! Never mind, it's all in a good cause.

Paperbacks abound at jumble sales and should not be despised. Tucked between the Zane Greys the writer recently picked up Bishop's *Winged Warfare* 1938 Penguin edition in almost mint condition — for the sum of 2p!

Book selection and values

Of all the air reference books undoubtedly the most famous is Jane's *All the World's Aircraft,* published annually, which, with advertisements, runs to around a thousand pages and costs £50 for the 1982/83 edition. Some of the older copies, once sold at a few guineas, now rate higher than the current copy. Some years have lost their high value in recent times due to reprints, for example David and Charles in 1972 re-published the 1938 Jane's at

£12.60. On the other hand there are vintage years, these being the 1919 and 1945/46 editions which, coming at the end of world wars and a long period of censorship, carry a mass of released information on aircraft of the war years. The character of Jane's has changed greatly over the years. The general sections on the air forces and civil aviation in each country was given up in the 1950s, and it appears to leave a gap that a new year-book could well fill. On the other hand, under earlier editors, Jane's was rarely as explicit on mark numbers and variants as it is today under John W. R. Taylor.

For historical reference, the Putnam aeronautical series are unrivalled in quality and scope and are standard works of reference. An excellent coverage is given of many of the famous constructors of the past, detailing type-by-type their productions. Firms covered so far are Airspeed, Armstrong Whitworth, Avro, Blackburn, Bristol, Curtiss, de Havilland, Fairey, Gloster, Handley Page, Hawker, Miles, Shorts, Sopwith, Supermarine and Vickers. Current firms covered are Boeing, Lockheed and McDonnell Douglas but in these cases, of course, only their products up to the time of publication can be included, so that updating will be necessary.

One aspect that publishers could well look to when producing such series, is some uniformity in dust covers, particularly the spine, so that book collectors who use protective plastic covers over the dust covers can proudly and neatly display their collection on shelves.

The value of books can fluctuate. A book on Japanese aircraft was published in 1945 in large quantity, but with the end of the war, aircraft book sales went down and eventually the publisher sold his large stocks for pulping, only to find a few years later that the book would sell at twice its original price.

Certain books have great value because of their limited print, like the manuscript of Albert E. Cowton, who served on RNAS balloons in World War 1 and later in the RAF on the North-West Frontier of India, which was published privately in limited numbers by his widow. The popular wartime series *Aircraft of the Fighting Powers* went to seven volumes, but due to a drop in postwar sales, there was a reduced print of the last two volumes, VI and VII, making them collectors' items in the 1960s and 1970s until facsimile editions of the two volumes appeared in 1979. Now collectors seek the earlier ones!

Squadron histories are sought by collectors, but apparently not by the general reader. Attempts to market these have usually failed. One of the most sought books in this field, and which will no doubt be selected for reprint, is *Over the Balkans and South Russia — Being the History of No 47 Squadron, RAF*, published in 1923, price 10/6d. Beaumont Aviation Literature tried to get the ball rolling in 1966 with *43 Squadron*, a fine work, but no other squadron histories ensued. Macdonalds took it up in the 1970s but gave it up after three books — *Twice Vertical* (No 1 Squadron), *The Flying Elephants* (No 27 Squadron) and *The Story of No 609 Squadron*. As it is, most published unit histories have appeared as articles in magazines, or limited print private publications.

Aircraft type histories

One of the largest demands is for aircraft type history books. In the early 1960s, the Macdonald Aircraft Monographs were started, but after *Hawker*

Hurricane, Gloster Gladiator and *Gloster Meteor* the series stopped. Yet sales by other publishers of this type of book continued. Fabers produced *Mosquito* and *Stirling* and Harleyford did *Spitfire* and *Lancaster.* Ian Allan have their *At War* and *Special* series. Patrick Stephens had their *Classic Aircraft* series, plus histories of the Hurricane and Harrier. Other series are continuing. In soft covers both Ducimus and Almark have produced type histories, eg *Supermarine Spitfire* and *Avro Anson Mks I, III, IV & X* respectively. This means that collectors of type histories have books of various styles, shapes and sizes.

In the booklet type of presentation there was the magnificent Profile series which ran to 258 different issues, each on a different aircraft type, produced throughout the 1960s and stopping in 1973. That such a popular series stopped was a blow to a large readership who could not understand why a series in such demand should fail. But there were difficulties through fluctuating demands such as between a well-known World War 2 aircraft and an obscure Polish type. Some bookshops regarded Profiles as magazines offering little profit per copy, and on the other hand they were not really periodicals with a steady sale per issue suitable for newsagents. Here is a case of the middle-man influencing the way you get the products you want. This is being countered by some small firms offering excellent soft-covered monographs on a postal sales basis; so cutting out the middle-man altogether. However, some Profiles are now being reprinted.

An Australian company, Kookaburra, started an aircraft type booklet series, using British authors, and this series has expanded into other subjects and larger books.

The publishing world now seems to be in a dilemma over type histories. There is a need for comprehensive books on the less familiar aircraft types. They have, no doubt, already been drafted, but with publishing costs today, to present such books comparable to the best of the monographs would mean a very high selling price and thereby limited sales. On the other hand the small booklet has marketing difficulties. Two firms have compromised by currently producing moderately priced books on aircraft types. One series is linked to the model market and the other to titling some of the less well-known aircraft types. It remains to be seen if books that cover new ground market better than the well-known names on which books have already been written. With a revival of interest in World War 1 aircraft a new field may be opening for aircraft type series. Of all the various types of aeronautical books, it is the aircraft type histories that collectors appear to treasure most, judging by publishers' print figures. Meanwhile, many books continue to be churned out which merely duplicate earlier works and have no evidence of original research.

Magazines

Most enthusiasts take a monthly magazine and/or the fortnightly *Aviation News.* For industry and the enthusiast who requires a weekly briefing there is *Flight International.* Many collectors keep complete runs of these books and, as advertisements show, will pay £1 a copy to make up a set. One of the largest holders of book copies of aeronautical magazines of all kinds is Beaumont's Aviation Literature already mentioned.

Magazines get soiled over the years and it is the bound copies that are most sought. A complete bound set of *Flight* from 1911 could command a four-figure sum. Odd copies of any magazine are of little saleable value, except to a buyer making up a set. But there are exceptions. A first copy of *Flight*, January 2 1909, price 1d (1½d post free) would be worth £25. World War 1 issues command the best prices and there were as many aeronautical periodicals as today — in 1919 *Aeronautics*, *Aeroplane* and *Flight*, all with 16 pages for 6d, appeared weekly, as did the 3d *Flying* and the 6d *Car & Aviatics*. Due to the waste paper appeals in World War 2, few copies have survived and bound copies appear on very few library shelves.

Catalogues of periodicals published can be found in aviation yearbooks, but there is no catalogue for aircraft works magazines which have often contained historical previews of their activities. North American Aviation produced a particularly fine periodical during World War 2, showing many of its products, Mitchells, Harvards and Mustangs, in the field.

Magazines are not as durable as books and once out of print are difficult to obtain. Most current magazine proprietors have a back copy service, but little reduction can be expected for out-of-date copies. The fact that they have taken up warehouse space for a period, taken office and warehousemen's time in replying and locating, means that they cannot be sold cheaply just because they are out of date. Magazines, like books, can grow in value with the passage of years.

Personal records and relics

Some enthusiasts are more interested in the personal aspects of aeronautics. Autobiographies and biographies of airmen have always attracted a large following of readership; there was a spate of books — the Hamilton series — shortly before World War 2 and currently personal narratives are to the fore in publishers' lists. It is a sad fact that many of the airmen who survived the major conflicts are now dying off. The historical value of their personal records such as log books, photo albums and photographs, may not be realised by their next of kin and be destroyed. Often they do not themselves realise the interest others would have in their personal records. The writer recalls one ex-RNAS Warrant Officer with a magnificent album of photographs taken at Eastchurch 1913-1919, who put it on a bonfire when he moved to smaller accommodation.

How to save this destruction of records can be a very delicate matter. It would be heartless to intrude on a bereaved family when the death of a veteran airman comes to notice, and after the passage of time it might be too late to save records. Approaches are best made while these veterans are still among us, but then they are prone to the unscrupulous collector who may try and wheedle records of which the airman is loath to part or be apprehensive about lending. The best service any enthusiast can do is to make the holder aware of the historical value of his items and that the Imperial War Museum, RAF or Fleet Air Arm Museum, or a local museum as appropriate, would be interested.

It is not just aircrew but aircraft designers and manufacturers that attract interest. In 1976 an exhibition hall was opened in Southampton to the memory of R. J. Mitchell, the chief designer of Supermarine, and biographies have appeared on the famous founders of aeronautical works such as de Havilland and Sopwith.

Log books

The basic record of flights kept by service aircrew was, and is, the flying log book. RNAS pilots logged their flights in Pilot's Flying Log Book S1516 introduced February 1915, revised September 1917, and RFC pilots in Army Book 425. When the two services amalgamated in 1918 the Army Book 425 format was adopted as RAF Book 425 (changed to Form 414 in the late 1920s) Flying Log Book. The essentials were a book maintained by each service pilot, and extended to all aircrew in late 1931, showing dates and times of flights (take-off and landing), identity of aircraft (serial number) pilot or passenger(s) and nature of duty. A separate book, Form 1767, was introduced later for aircrew.

These are prime documents. They are invaluable to a biographer of an airman and have been an aid to many an autobiography. The remarks added in these books include many incidents not officially recorded elsewhere. The log book of a famous pilot such as an ace of World War 1 would fetch several hundred pounds in auction. They have become collectors' items and some enthusiasts, interested in the information they contain, have taken facsimiles of logs held by ex-Service pilots. Log books are items much prized by their compilers and it is sad to relate that some collectors have caused distress to some old World War 1 pilots by borrowing log books and not returning them.

Inevitably, there are some anomalies. The RNAS and RFC ruling was that S1516 and Book 425 would be kept by all flying ranks junior to Squadron Commander/Major. The RAF ruling was RAF Book 425 would be kept by every officer of the General Duties Branch below the rank of Wing Commander, changed to every pilot below the rank of Group Captain in October 1932. This has meant over the years that many flights by senior officers have gone unlogged, and similarly those by officers of other branches — one medical officer, for example, comes near to holding the World War 2 record for the number of operational sorties. Some pilots wrote almost a narrative in their logs and included photos pasted on the pages, others were brief. Aircraft identities, which correctly should be the aircraft serial numbers, were sometimes given by unit letter only, or the serial figures without quoting the prefix letters — even a combination of the unit letter and the serial number has been noted in more than one log.

There are thousands of log books around, most service pilots from pre-World War 1 and aircrew from World War 2 kept their flying or aircrew log books. While the books are official documents they may, as an act of grace as the regulations put it, be retained by individuals. As the veterans die, so many of these records are thrown away. Tens of thousands were destroyed officially in the 1960s. There were stacks of log books from aircrew missing in World War 2 which, in a number of cases, included their pre-war and even World War 1 logs. Notices were put in the press for next of kin to claim, but few were requested. A relatively small number have been preserved and are held by the Public Record Office catalogued under AIR 4.

Recording recollections

Sounds of the past are now part of aeronautica. There are records on sale that recall the sound of, for example, Merlin engines in the same way that the railway enthusiasts have their sound records of steam engines. A new trend in recent years has been to record on tape the experiences of pioneer and World War 1 pilots and aircrew. The Imperial War Museum has made a collection of such recollections in recent years. There are still hundreds of survivors, but whose numbers dwindle weekly.

Those who know of such old-timers and wish to tape their recollections should be forewarned of the difficulties of fruitful recording in this way. Memories can play odd tricks with scant regard for what actually happened. After the passage of 60 years, minds become blurred and often what is said is not what was experienced, but what subsequently the man being interviewed has read of the great conflict. Much time and tape can be wasted in waffling, to no historical advantage whatsoever. It is also easy to offend. The writer had one man convinced that he flew Sopwith Camels operationally in 1916 and who took it as a personal affront when told that the Camel did not go into service until 1917. He was there — and he knew! One highly decorated pilot, who came to see the writer following a review of his book in which facts were challenged, confessed that he got 'old so-and-so' to write up his experiences and genuinely believed that it was factually recorded.

To interview, elementary psychology must be used. Talking generally will almost inevitably have a nebulous result. You must go from the known to the unknown. Any documentation, photographs and in particular log books are good starting points. Initial questions from log book entry or photos should be testing questions on subjects known to the interviewer; then when satisfied that memory has not been impaired the interviewer can follow through with questions asking for expansion of detail in log book remarks column, or about people in photographs.

Unless a very senior officer is being interviewed it is pointless to talk of strategies. Participants knew little of policies at the time, and tactics are best limited to personal tactics. Only post-war did the majority of service-men find out from books how the part they played fitted into the war planning. Beware of adding to the distorted facts of history from spoken words — there are quite enough in the written word!

Techniques used by British television in historical presentations have often involved famous personalities of the air giving their recollections. In general, these are not so revealing as it may appear. They result largely from books the programme researchers have consulted, following which the personalities concerned are contacted and filmed giving quotations from their own works which have been on the library shelves for many years. They tend too, to give a rather false impression. When time has taken its toll, it is difficult to accept the halting speech and frail appearance as coming from the men of action they undoubtedly were. It is far more important to preserve, and show when occasion demands, film or recorded comments of such personalities at the time, than showing them as they are now.

Lectures and forums

In these days of television, the visiting lecturer has lost some of his appeal but there are some very interesting lecturers on circuit. Major A. P. de Jong and Gerrit Zwanenburg lecture in Britain at periods on their work in investigating the hundreds of wrecks recovered in Dutch land reclamation. Roger Freeman, the well-known author specialising in the USAAF in Britain, lectures both at home and abroad. The great advantage of the visiting lecturer is, of course, the opportunity to put your own questions. In this connection the Annual Test Pilots' Forum, which Charles W. Cain has been arranging for over 20 years for the London Society of Air Britain, is both popular and unique. Here at the Caxton Hall famous test pilots face a barrage of questions that society members place.

There are some very interesting lectures on aeronautical themes on television, but unlike formal lectures such as at the Royal Aeronautical Society (which, incidentally, non-members can attend as guests or by arrangement), there is little advance notice. While the actual lecture may have been filmed and recorded months previously, its showing is decided only weeks prior to presentation. Advance notification would be helpful, but this would affect exclusive arrangements with the *Radio Times* and *TV Times*. In any case, a presentation once scheduled in these magazines, does not guarantee showing. Current events may well intervene, and the historical always has to give way to the topical.

Flight International, the famous British aeronautical weekly, normally gives a good service in advance notification of most aeronautical events including important lectures in this field.

Essays and manuscripts

Some of the most revealing historical writings have appeared in essay form and many of these, as apart from articles, have not been published.

Among some of the most interesting essays were those produced by RAF Staff College students between the two wars. The college opened at Andover in 1922 under Air Vice-Marshal R. M. Brooke-Popham who instituted a lecture or essay by each student relating to their experiences during their service. These were no ordinary students, to quote but a few that year — Wing Commander J. E. A. Baldwin, DSO, OBE and R. E. C. Peirse, DSO, AFC; Squadron Leaders W. Sholto Douglas MC, DFC; C. F. A. Portal DSO, MC and K. R. Park MC, DFC. For the years 1923-24 and 1924-25 a selection was published as Air Publications (AP1097 and AP 1152 respectively). These were for official use only and were not seen by the general public, but they are available for perusal at the Public Record Office and any other such essays not included in APs by Staff College Students are well worth tracing. If only they had all written autobiographies.

One of the finest collections of essays was undoubtedly the Royal Aeronautical Society's *Centenary Journal 1866-1966.* This 300-page January 1966 issue (Vol 70 No 661) of the *Journal* of the Royal Aeronautical Society contains some 75 essays on aeronautical aspects by such persons as Sir Sidney Camm, Sir Alan Cobham, Sir George Dowty, Sir Roy Fedden, R. Hafner, J. D. North, etc.

Many unpublished manuscripts make a valuable contribution to historical records and many such works are held at the Imperial War Museum — for example Basil Catchpole's detailed treatise on Army Co-operation work 1917-18. Such manuscripts are too technical and detailed to appeal to the general reader so that general publication is not practical. Most publishers will not consider a work commercially viable unless it warrants a print of at least 3,000 copies.

Richthofen relics

Personal relics of famous airmen are among the most prized forms of aeronautics. The most famous of all are, no doubt, those associated with Manfred von Richthofen, the German ace of aces of World War 1. Relics of his final triplane are scattered far and wide. The largest piece, the Oberursel engine, is in the Imperial War Museum, London. Other parts are held by national museums in Australia and Canada, so emphasising the controversy as to who did shoot von Richthofen down — the Australian ground gunners or the Canadian pilot Captain Roy Brown of No 209 Squadron, RAF.

Quite a number of enthusiasts have made Richthofen alone their study, reading all they can of this famous German and collecting every photograph having bearing upon his activities. In one book alone (*von Richthofen and the Flying Circus*, Argus Books) Richthofen himself appears in 60 different settings among the 250 photos.

There are two areas open for research which require investigation on the Continent that some enthusiasts might combine with a holiday if they can get the necessary permits. The first concerns the Richthofen Museum at Schweinitz, first started by his family in his house wherein were placed the relics of the aircraft he shot down and the silver cups he had made for his first 64 victories. When the Russians advanced through Silesia in 1944, the family fled taking only a few treasured mementos. What has happened to these relics?

The second aspect concerns the research still to be done on Richthofen's flying life of which only a fraction is documented. All the books concentrate on the 80 flights in which Richthofen achieved victories, and for which combat reports exist. But in aerial warfare more fights are inconclusive than conclusive; so what of the hundred or so brushes Richthofen must have had to achieve 80 victories, and the even larger number when no enemy was sighted? These have never been documented.

The churchyard at Bertangles where Richthofen was first buried, featured in so many photographs, remains unchanged after all these years, but the propeller headstone disppeared. His present resting place is the Richthofen tomb in the Invaliden cemetery, now in the Russian zone of Berlin.

Autographs

Autograph hunting is a general hobby and older than aeronautics, but in modern times a few collectors have restricted themselves to autographs connected with aeronautics for the scope is wide with aces, air pioneers, Service leaders, test pilots, record breakers, manufacturers, etc. There are probably many highly valued autographs in the files of many enthusiasts, who may be unaware of their value. The autographs of aces like Richthofen, Ball and Mannock or record-breakers like Alcock and Brown, would rate now around £100. On the other hand the signature of one of the highest scoring aces of World War 1, Raymond Collishaw, would barely rate £1 for the simple reason that Air Vice-Marshal Collishaw carried on between the wars and through World War 2 writing reports, letters and minutes, and was then a most prolific writer until he died. Facsimiles are practically worthless, but are included by collectors interested in calligraphy, against the day when a genuine signature will turn up.

Signed photographs of personalities are much sought by some collectors. While signatures are preferred, initialling is usually acceptable where it constituted a form of signature, for example Trenchard, who would sign *H. M. Trenchard* in his early days, would rarely go beyond *T* when Chief of the Air Staff. In such cases collectors prefer the initialling to be a handwritten text for its calligraphical interest.

Some of the most treasured items of aeronautica are the signed menu cards of reunions. Some squadrons have held reunions annually since World War 1 and there have been meetings of VCs, 'Old Eagles', aircraft firms, test pilots, etc, at which dinner played an important part of the function and menu cards were passed round the table for all to sign.

Among my souvenirs

The scope of aeronautica is wide, just how wide is indicated by a recent sale at Christie's of motoring, aeronautical, etc, material. Items included *Notes on Aerial Fighting* issued by the Air Council in 1918, 15 copies of the *Aeromodeller* 1960-62, a Roy Nockolds painting of the trans-Atlantic Vickers Vimy, a dry point etching of the Graf Zeppelin by Geoffrey Watson, an album of 100 negatives of World War 1, a navigator's map-reading lamp said to be from a Wellington and a Lang propeller circa 1916. Many such items are reviewed in this section.

Medals

The collecting of medals is more militaria than aeronautica, and it is now a very expensive hobby. There is, too, something rather pathetic about national awards changing hands, as it often implies that the recipient is dead and that those bequeathed the medals did not regard them with family pride. On the other hand, most collectors are cognisant of the sentiments involved, and take an avid interest in the life and deeds of the men and women whose awards they hold. Many collections have started by adding to awards proudly kept by a family.

The 1914-20 War and 1914-18 Victory medals and the Campaign stars of the 1939-1945 War are the most easily acquired as they were a general issue to all who served in the various campaigns as apart from those decorations and medals awarded to individuals for special acts. Of the campaign medals, one was issued exclusively to aircrew — the Air Crew Europe Star. The RAF has, too, its own Long Service and Good Conduct and Meritorious Service medals. Some might consider the Royal Observer Corps medal as aeronautica since the ROC functionally counts as an RAF Group. Less well known and well down in the Order of Precedence, but sought by collectors, are the Air Efficiency Award and Queen's Medal for Champion Shots of the Air Forces.

The variety of medals that could be considered as aeronautica runs into hundreds when all aspects are considered; to quote a few: Naval awards to Royal Naval Air Service personnel, the Vietnam Medal awarded *inter alia* to Royal Australian Air Force and Royal New Zealand Air Force crew who served in Vietnam, the foreign decorations bestowed on airmen by Allies during the two world wars, and more recently by the late Government of Vietnam to RAAF and RNZAF personnel.

The gems of medal collections are, of course, the VCs; particularly the air VCs because they are so well known. There is, however, little chance of these medals coming on to the market, and if they did the going price would be around £6,500. Of the air medals, the following is the minimum 1975 price a London firm would pay for examples: Distinguished Flying Cross World War 1 — £70; World War 2 — £35; post World War 2 — £55. Distinguished Flying Medal World War 1 — £125; World War 2 — £44; post World War 2 — £130. Air Force Cross — £55. Air Force Medal — £65.

The factors that condition prices are, of course, the availability. There were fewer NCO pilots in World War 1, and few recipients ever sell their own medals, so that it is not the older medals that get the higher prices.

An aspect of medal collecting is obtaining the complete row of medals awarded to an individual; most recipients of gallantry awards would have campaign medals and some individuals an imposing 'clutch'. It is not always the number of decorations but the circumstances. A particularly unusual 'clutch' was that of Wing Commander Frank H. Kirby VC, OBE, DCM who gained his honours before he came into the RAF. A single medal can have particular value such as the Military Medal awarded to Sergeant Patrick Colgan, RAF, which is normally exclusive to Army personnel. Sergeant Colgan was an attached member of the Sea Reconnaissance Unit of the Royal Navy who, as a frogman, materially assisted in establishing a bridgehead over the Irrawaddy cutting barbed wire under fire and swam the river to get medical supplies.

With the high value placed on medals, there is a security problem, but thieves would find it difficult to dispose of the valuable medals. While campaign medals of World War 2, for example, are not identifiable with any individual, medals from the General Service Medal upwards bear name, initials and number of the recipient. These may be ground out, but the true collectors are concerned with the identity of the recipient.

Collecting medal ribbons is much more within the pockets of all. The ribbons of most honours, decorations and awards are held by military tailors and are sold by the inch (or by centimetres now) in some shops for a matter of pence. They make a very colourful and attractive display for a modest sum. Taking in consideration all the countries of the world, the Orders and Medals Research Society record some 28,000 medal ribbons of which several thousand have relevance to airmen or a connection with aviation. They are being continually added to, for example since UDI Rhodesia has introduced 32 new awards.

As an illustrated introduction to British Medals, *The Observer's Book of British Awards & Medals*, by Edward C. Joslin is published by Frederick Warne. A more comprehensive reference work is *Ribbons & Medals* by Taprell Dorling ('Taffrail').

Unit badge collecting

Collecting RAF unit badges is a hobby of many, judging from correspondence on the subject. This is not the collection of the actual badge for there is only one and it bears the Sovereign's signature, but the collection of an impression of each badge. These date from 1936. Prior to that date units adopted badges on a parochial basis. From 1936, in order to put RAF badges on a similar footing to regimental colours, King Edward VIII was asked if he would personally examine and approve each badge. The Mas-

Left *Imperial Crown,* **centre** *St Edward's Crown,* **top right** *Naval Crown and* **bottom right** *Astral Crown.*

ter Sketches, approved by Chester Herald, are recorded by the College of Heralds, and some have been framed and retained by squadrons. The royal approval to badges was also extended to Commonwealth Air Forces.

The official badges are contained within a set frame as illustrated, but variations are in frame shape for some Commonwealth units and the St Edward's Crown differs from the Imperial Crown at the head of the frame. If a unit disbanded before the Queen came to the throne in 1952 then the Imperial Crown applied and to units in being from 1952 St Edward's Crown appertains. There is also the Naval Crown which is used with Fleet Air Arm units and the Astral Crown which surmounts, for example, the ATC badge.

The badges are loosely called squadron badges, but the official RAF badges include Commands, Groups, stations, schools, depots and units as well as squadron badges. So far there is no published guide to the full list of badges issued, but an indication of the scope can be found in the badges in the aisles of St Clement Danes, the church of the RAF.

Players cigarettes in 1937 whetted the appetite with a set of 50 cards of RAF badges in colour with text explaining the origin of the devices depicted, and sets can still be bought for under £5, proving how avidly they were collected at the time for so many sets to survive and so keeping the price down. Black and white representation of RAF badges can be found in various works, eg

Title	Publisher	Badges
Bomber Squadrons of the RAF	Macdonald	176
Fighter Squadrons of the RAF	Macdonald	195
Aircraft Camouflage and Markings 1907-1954	Harleyford	400
Aircraft Markings of the World 1912-1967	Harleyford	95

Unfortunately the following *Coastal Command Squadrons of the RAF* did not feature badge illustrations due to the high reproduction fees required by the Ministry of Defence.

The Royal Air Force Museum sells enamelled miniature squadron badges. In late 1982 the scope was Squadron Nos. 1-72, 74-35, 41-52, 55-60, 64-72, 74-75, 79, 83-85, 88, 92, 98-100, 104, 115, 120, 121, 201, 202-209, 216 and 617. These were priced (1982) at 75p each.

Wall plaques of squadron and other unit badges are available at some West End jewellers. The famous firm of Skinner & Co, for example, specialises as aviation jewellers and silversmiths and offers a 9½ × 6½ wall plaque of unit badges at under £10 per badge. This would, of course, make a collection expensive, but these are items of aeronautica suitable for presentation to ex-members of the squadron.

A photographic print of squadron and unit badges is held by the Ministry of Defence (Reprographic Services), King Charles Street, London, SW1, and copies can be obtained for special purposes.

Not for collection, but for contemplation, are some 800 RAF unit badges sculptured and embedded in the floor of the aisle at St Clement Danes, the Central Church of the RAF. But strangely, although brass-rubbings in churches is a pastime of some antiquarians, badge stone-rubbing has not yet become an air enthusiasts' pastime at St Clement Danes.

The greatest work on squadron badges has yet to appear. Miss J. H. Alexander and Mr Sidney Bostock have, with the full permission of the Ministry of Defence, made an exhaustive study of the origin of unit badges and have collected a pictorial representation, in colour where possible, of every badge approved up to 1968. It is hoped that the fruits of their labours are soon to be published.

American squadron badges, Air Force, Navy and Marine Corps, are complicated by changing form with changing roles. French escadrille markings have remained fairly consistent. Three books dealing with Chasse (fighter), Bombardment and Reconnaissance Units were published in France in the mid-1950s illustrating the badges in colour and have now become valuable collectors' items. Articles and illustrations on Federal German, Italian, Danish, Dutch and Norwegian squadron markings have appeared in recent years in the various aeronautical monthlies.

It is not just the acquisition of the badges that fascinates, but the story behind the unit's adoption of a particular motif. Aeronautica and records cannot be divorced from each other if the most is to be made of collecting.

Trade marks and letterheads

There is no public scheme for the preservation of records of commercial aviation firms, and since World War 2, in the case of America and Britain, and from just before World War 2 in the case of France and Germany, there have been so many changes in the aircraft industry that many famous manufacturers have lost their identity — Avro, Bristol, Curtiss, Fairey, Gloster, Hanriot, Junkers, North American, Supermarine and Vought — to quote but a few. Each firm had a distinctive trademark usually incorporated in their letterheads and marked on their products.

The range of trade marks is quite wide when all countries of the world are considered over the years. Examples of many can be seen in the advertisement pages of *Jane's All the World's Aircraft* and aeronautical magazines, particularly the unbound copies of the latter. However, except

Letterheads of some aeronautical companies.

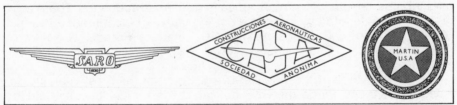

on covers and supplements, the trade marks were rarely in colour; but most firms splashed out with expensive letterheads, Auster in particular having a large badge in gold colouring. Items of correspondence with these firms have thereby become prized items of aeronautica.

The badges/trade marks were often marked on the outboard side of outer interwing struts on World War 1 biplanes which brings many sub-contractors into the field, like Standard Motors whose Union Jack trademark appeared on the struts of Sopwith Pups. As these were transfers that were varnished over, a few genuine examples have survived and the golden Auster badge may be seen in the cockpits of a number of light aircraft still flying.

Aerial leaflets

Among the most treasured items of aeronautica are the genuine aerial leaflets; papers produced for distribution by dropping from the air. These date back to the days of ballooning when events were advertised by dropping leaflets — now an offence against the law.

The use of leaflets for propaganda proved effective during World War 1 and hundreds of different leaflets were dropped in the various theatres. In the inter-war years, thousands of leaflets in various native dialects were dropped as warnings when the RAF were forced to take punitive action against recalcitrant tribes; all are of interest to collectors.

A vast increase in the types of leaflets dropped came during World War 2 in which RAF leaflet raids went under the code-name of 'Nickels'. From 1939 onwards the Allies dropped millions of leaflets of thousands of different types by aircraft, and by 'M' Balloon Unit when winds were suitable.

Leaflets during World War 2 were distributed for two main reasons; to demoralise our enemies and to elate our Allies, and they become more effective as the war went on. In November 1943 alone, 63,150,970 leaflets were dropped by the Allies. Yet, strangely, although the leaflets were for the enemy, or for our allies in occupied countries which the enemy could not but fail to see, the leaflet contents were not revealed to the British public at the time. Most leaflets that survived were those surreptitiously pocketed by aircrew as souvenirs or to show to family and friends who were naturally curious, and who could see no harm in knowing what the Germans could see.

The leaflets averaged 6 × 9 inches in size and in general were of poor quality paper. Uncollected, they were soon pulped by rain, dew and mist. In late 1944 leaflet bombs were used in a bomb cluster container, set to explode in the air and scatter the leaflets. Some which did not explode may still be deep in soft ground, but since a standard American M-17 bomb casing was used, it would be difficult now to tell whether the case contained leaflets or bombphlets!

Leaflets of each different print dropped on Europe by the Allies were serial numbered, but were not dropped in numerical sequence. There were various series denoted by a prefix letter indicative of the intended destination: B-Belgium, C-Czechoslovakia, D-Denmark, F-France, G-Germany, H-Holland, I-Italy, J-Channel Isles (Jersey etc), L-Luxembourg, N-Norway and P-Poland.

The current value of these leaflets vary. Some of the most valuable are those never used. Since the RAF delivered the goods, the Air Ministry reserved the right to veto deliveries if the type of propaganda could bring reprisals on captured aircrew. Some leaflets were suppressed and, official-ly, all copies destroyed. It is the few of such batches that survived that now command good prices. Counter leaflets are also among the most valuable. The Germans dropped leaflets over occupied countries giving false news, making it appear that the papers were a product of the Allies. In turn the Allies had to drop leaflets to warn of the false leaflets. False money, clo-thing and ration cards were also dropped over Germany in an attempt to disrupt their economy.

Examples of wartime leaflets are — F19, French Air Force in Action, with photos of the Lorraine Squadron and F177, a collection of French songs regularly broadcast by the BBC, dropped over France in March 1944, fol-lowed the next month by F45 being a speech by Lord Vansittart on the 40th Anniversary of the *Entente Cordiale.* A significant leaflet, distributed late 1943 over wide areas of Germany, was G101 titled 'Who Was Right?', it contained extracts of speeches by Winston Churchill and Air Chief Marshal Harris conflicting with those of Goebbels and Goering. This was followed by G11 in March 1944 warning the German peoples that the air offensive would reach a scale beyond anything yet imagined. A typical American leaflet was USF110 titled 'The Voice of America' notifying the French of a new American radio station in Great Britain and stating wavelengths and transmission times. Canada entered the field with CF1, reporting a speech delivered by General de Gaulle in Canada for the benefit of the occupied French.

In India hundreds of different leaflets were prepared for dropping to the Japanese, and post-war over Malaya leaflets were dropped to the Com-munist terrorists in the jungle. In some parts of the world, leaflets from the air are still a method of communication today. The field is very wide and so far not many collectors are in the field, but this is a subject in which interest will grow for so little has been published on the subject and, as far as is known, no comprehensive catalogue of leaflets has been published.

Prices, of course, vary greatly. The most common leaflets will fetch at least £1 and for such unusual items as leaflets dropped by HMS *Dunedin's* aircraft on Samoa in February 1930 during the Mau insurrection, at least £10. But the real gems are the World War 1 forged newspapers with false news dropped by aircraft which can fetch up to £100 per item.

Displaying a collection is rather difficult for, unlike stamps, leaflets were often double-sided to make the most use of the paper. Most collectors keep them in albums with hinged transparent envelopes. It is, of course, essential to keep the leaflets flat to prevent deterioration through creasing and, understandably, the paper was of poor quality as their intended use was ephemeral. Also, unlike stamps no franking was involved so that there is no check on whether or not a leaflet was actually dropped. Because of this a mint copy, extracted from a bale before dropping, is just as valuable as one collected on the ground.

A booklet on aerial propaganda leaflets was published by Francis J. Field Ltd in the 1950s and copies now rate over £5 to £10 second-hand according to condition.

Stamps

The most popular of all hobbies is philately and some aspects of this can be regarded as aeronautica, in particular air mail stamps. In Britain there are no air mail stamps, normal stamps being used to the correct denomination for mail by air with an air mail label; but in many countries, including the USA, there are special stamps for air mail and some enthusiasts collect just these. The range is wide with air mail stamps being issued by many countries from the 1920s to today. Some countries made ordinary stamps into air mail ones by overprinting, in some cases with an aircraft silhouette. While some countries had simple designs, often featuring wings, others portrayed actual aircraft types. The possibilities run into thousands with values varying from 1p to over £100 each.

Apart from the air mail stamps, there are many ordinary stamps with aircraft connections. To give but a few examples to show the scope: in 1970 Australia portrayed aircraft old and new in a series to commemorate the 50th anniversary of Qantas. Britain had six different 4d stamps alone for the Battle of Britain anniversary and there have been RAF formation and first non-stop Atlantic flight anniversary issues, Concorde stamps, etc. France in recent years has featured aircraft types such as the MS760 Paris, Noratlas and Mystere 20, as well as famous airmen and airwomen. Hungary in 1967 issued a series showing an aeronautical past from 1617 — where else could you find an image of the Horváth Ernö monoplane of 1911 or the PKZ-2 helicopter of 1918? Russia has issued several series of stamps showing aircraft and if the aeronautical theme is extended to astronautics then not only Russia, but even countries like Dominica celebrate on stamps *Conquista de Espacio* — the conquest of space.

Many stamp collectors now limit collections to a group of countries or even a single country because the range of different stamps is so vast. So others limit their collections to air mails or those with aeronautical associations.

Postal covers

A relatively new off-shoot of philately is that of postal cover collecting, many of which have an aeronautical theme due largely to RAF efforts to support the magnificent RAF Museum. There had been interest for some years in obtaining new stamps used on the first day of issue. Dealers arranging direct post to customers went a step further in having a special envelope marked appropriate to the event being commemorated in the new issues, and not a few were aeronautical themes. The RAF, following an Army lead, went further and arranged various ingenious deliveries, with Post Office approval, using veteran aircraft, current service aircraft, parachuting, etc, with envelopes marked up attractively with some event from RAF history.

Some cover collectors include the normal envelopes of airlines and aircraft manufacturers, and of special events. In 1968, for example, colourful envelopes were produced in their thousands to celebrate the joint Golden Jubilee of the RAF and Silver Jubilee of the RAF Association.

Cover collecting is a growing hobby and since the value of the covers, like those of stamps, rises over the years, some people are acquiring them as an investment.

Picture postcards

In the realm of collectors, picture postcards are claimed as having the third widest interest; stamp and coin collecting taking pride of place. Certainly postcards are items in which many antique dealers now trade and there are a number of establishments that trade exclusively in postcards and even postcard fairs are held.

As interest increases, with more collectors entering the field, prices rise and in recent years far faster than the rate of inflation. Some individual cards are actually fetching 100 times their value ten years ago.

Sending picture cards as a general means of correspondence started on the Continent and reached Britain in late Victorian times, circa 1895. The craze caught on rapidly and the heyday of the postcard was from the turn of the century to World War 1. Thousands of photographers and artists were commissioned to meet the public demand for correspondence in this form, when both cost of card and postage could be sent for one penny (old pence). These were the pioneer days of aviation and aircraft featured among other subjects. Hundreds of cards were printed of aviation meetings, the *Daily Mail* Tour of 1912, airmen of the day and aerial views. Such cards now rate good prices. A man at Sutton Coldfield advertised in 1975: 'Wanted. Up to £200+ paid for early Balloon & Aeroplane cards: others used before 1914 from £1 to £100 each.'

To the general collector cards that have been actually used as correspondence is an important aspect, but to the aeronautical enthusiast the acquisition of a new photograph is sufficient in itself and collecting aeronautical postcards is just a facet of the aircraft photo collector. In this respect they are also sought by authors of aircraft books and articles to help ring the changes in the presentation of photographs.

World War 1, with its upheaval of population, brought on a new spate of postcard issues for correspondence, featuring wartime subjects and, inevitably, including aviation. Some of these cards could be purchased from dealers at relatively low prices in the Charing Cross Road district of London in the 1970s, but prices there now are rather high.

Between the wars the card craze gradually gave way to the local interest pictures, such as seaside views for holidaymakers, but some of these included aerial views and even, on occasions, aircraft. Flips were given from local fields and even seafront floatplane flips. It was these aircraft that featured on the cards, either photographically or in art form. The air circuses of the 1930s had postcard sales in the admission tents and Sir Alan Cobham's Air Display ran a series of 50 postcards of aircraft in conjunction with Aerofilms.

RAF personnel stationed at home and abroad would often send home postcard pictures of aircraft, and some stations had souvenir cards printed. The aircraft of Halton featured on postcards by W. H. Christmas, Camp Photographer, Aylesbury Road, Wendover, Bucks. These were very fine sepia photographs with Postcard Correspondence/Address printed backings. He did not number his cards so there is no indication now of the extent of this magnificent collection. W. E. Mack of London NW3 issued a Sepia Satin Series in the 1930s which included aircraft subjects.

All the air photographs of the Imperial War Museum's collection were then available as postcards. A museum publication of 1938 stated: 'The collection of photographs of the Air Services in the Reference Departments of the Museum illustrates all sides of the work of the RFC, RNAS and RAF during the War of 1914-1918, and the more important types of aircraft used. There were also photographs of French, German and other Air Services, and of the damage caused by air raids. The collection of Air Photographs includes views of the whole of the British Western Front, and of other theatres of war, taken from the air.' The prices were listed as follows: Postcard reproductions of exhibits, 1d each. Postcard reproductions of paintings and drawings, 1d each. Postcard-photographs of types of ships, aircraft, tanks, guns, etc, to order, 6d each.

During World War 2, postcards were a non-essential which soon went by the board. Valentine and Sons Ltd of London and Dundee, one of the best-known producers of postcards, turned to the production of Valentines Aircraft Recognition Cards in conjunction with *The Aeroplane*. These cards, now another collectors' item, had a photo of an aircraft type one side and a three-view silhouette, data and recognition points on the other.

The interest engendered by the aviation during World War 2 led to an interest post-war in aircraft postcards, but as a collection, rather than for postal purposes. Real Photographs Ltd of Victoria House, Southport, met this need by producing a range of hundreds of aircraft photographs. As their popularity grew, regular catalogue check lists were published and even an *RP News*, edited by Captain Ellison Hawks, giving news of new acquisitions and containing correspondence about the subjects from enthusiastic collectors. The August 1946 catalogue of 'Aeroplane Photographs' (Price 1/-) offered over 3,000 subjects, all in 5½ × 3½ inch postcards at 7/- per dozen. While many were well-known published photos, there were some 1914-18 War and NW Frontier shots that were absolute gems.

For 12 years the list of subjects grew. The last list sent to the writer was the September/October 1956 duplicated sheet taking the collection up to A4258. But by this time the glossy and detailed 'Check Lists of our Aeroplane Photographs' which gave serials and camera angles had already become collectors' pieces, and often requests for earlier photos would meet with out-of-stock letters. There have been attempts to revive the collection in recent years, and the majority of the early photos are now collectors' items. Recently the writer came across some in a London shop off the Charing Cross Road, where prices were around 80p each! Some of the specialist aviation bookshops trade in these cards at a much more reasonable price.

In the early post-war days a collector could get postcard size photographs from the Imperial War Museum at costs only marginally more than pre-war. Visitors could then peruse the photo collection without prior appointment, fill in an order form and pay on delivery in a couple of weeks. There was a brisk trade and thousands of these postcard-sized photographs must be around the world and, when marketed today, are fetching a price much higher than the cost of a present-day print.

The art colour painting type of card had a limited revival post-war. In the 1950s J. Salmon Ltd of Sevenoaks published a series of airliner cards and followed it up with a series of British Warplanes cards which, in 1971, were published in book form as *'British Warplanes 1914-1954* — A Salmon Colour Book — 50 coloured illustrations'.

Many airlines have issued postcards on their aircraft, route maps and menus as a form of advertising, and these are now becoming collectors' items.

In general, aviation enthusiasts appear unaware of the interesting new photos to be found in postcard collections. There are some 50 main postcard dealers and many local antique shops will help. Some dealers provide comprehensive illustrated catalogues. It would, perhaps, be unfair to recommend one particular dealer but you can choose for yourself, many advertise regularly in the *Exchange & Mart,* available at newsagents.

Cigarette and trade cards

There were few boys in the years 1910-1939 who did not avidly collect cigarette cards. Not only were the cards aesthetically pleasing, they were often informative and an education in themselves. Then there was the thrill of collecting the full set with all that it involved in acquisition; the swopping of duplicates with one's schoolfriends, the searching of discarded packets, briefing uncles and indulging in the one form of begging that was not considered antisocial — 'Fagcard Mister?'.

For those interested in aircraft, there was plenty of scope in the 1930s. As early as 1910 W. D. & H. O. Wills brought out a series titled 'Aviation' (a misnomer as it contained lighter-than-air craft) issuing them in Britain, Australia and New Zealand. During World War 1 several series touched upon aeronautics, and Lambert & Butler in 1915 issued a small series of 25 exclusively on 'Aviation'. The early 1920s were lean years for the aircraft enthusiasts, but from 1926, until the paper economies of World War 2, one or another of the various cigarette brands were issuing cards on an aeronautical subject at a frequency exceeding a set a year. These were:

Year	Subject of series	Issued by	Set of
1926-8	Aerial Navigations (3 series)	Savoy Products	3×56
1927	Famous Aircraft	Amalgamated Press	16
1928	A Day on an Airway	Sarony and Co	25
1929	Types of Aeroplanes	Murray Cigarettes	25
1930	British Aircraft	Robertson & Woodcock	50
1932-3	History of Aviation (2 series)	Lambert & Butler	2×25
1933	Aircraft	UK Tobacco Co	50
1934	Aviation	R. & J. Hill	25
1935	Aeroplanes of Today	British American Tobacco	50
1935	Famous British Airmen and Airwomen	Lambert & Butler	25
1935	Aeroplanes (Civil)	John Player & Sons	50
1936	Famous Airmen and Airwomen	Carreras Ltd	50
1936	Empire Air Routes	Lambert & Butler	50
1936	International Air Liners	John Player & Sons	50
1936	Aeroplanes of Today	United Tobacco (SA)	50
1937	The RAF at Work	W. A. & A. C. Churchman	*48
1937	Aeroplane Markings	Lambert & Butler	50
1938	Flying	(Consortium issue)	*48
1938	Famous Aeroplanes, Pilots and Airports	Mars Confections	50
1938	Aircraft	Godfrey Phillips	54
1938	Aircraft of the RAF	John Player & Sons	50

Album for squadron badge cigarette cards issued 1937.

Year	Subject of series	Issued by	Set of
1938	British Aircraft	Strathmore Tobacco	*25
1939	Wings over the Empire	W. A. & A. C. Churchman	*48
1939	Aeroplanes	Gallaher Cigarettes	48
1939	Britain from the Air	J. A. Pattreiouex	*48

*These cards were larger than standard card size which normally was approximately 2⅝×1⅜ inches (68×36 mm).

Cherished by their owners, thousands of these cards are preserved. Being relatively small in bulk they escaped the ravages of the wartime waste paper collections. Hundreds of sets and thousands of loose cards come on to the market in present day house clearances. A 1976 card catalogue has such gems as Player's 'RAF Badges' and 'Aircraft of the RAF' at a modest £1.25 a set each. Dearer, but of particular interest, are the Ardath cigarette large cards — the 25 'Fighting and Civil Aircraft' issued in 1936, and 36 'Real Photographs of Modern Aircraft' of 1939 which now constitutes a collection of vintage aircraft photos; the market price of the pre-war sets varies from £4 upwards.

Post-war, even before the toxic effects of cigarettes were generally recognised, there was a shift from cigarettes to other items of trade for the issue of picture cards. The largest in size was the Master Vending Company issue of extra large cards of Jet Aircraft of the World with gum; with 100 cards in the series, and with due allowance for the duplicates, it was more than most people could chew! Smaller than standard were the 20 sets of cards the British Automatic Company issued with their weight machines, 1948-54, of which one set of 24 was titled 'British Aircraft'. Other card sets issued since World War 2 are:

Year	Subject of series	Issued by	Set of
1950	British Aircraft	British Auto	24
1951	Modern Aircraft	Beano Gum	50
1952	History of Aviation	Mills Cigarettes	*50

Year	Subject of series	Issued by	Set of
1953	Modern British Aircraft	J. J. Beaulah	24
1953	Fifty Years of Flying	Cadet Sweets	50
1953	British Aircraft	Turf Cigarettes	50
1953	British Planes	Morning Foods	25
1952	Modern Aircraft (2 series)	Osborne Tobacco	2×50
1954	Modern Aircraft	Sweetule Products	50
1955	Aircraft of Today	Mitchum Foods	25
1956	Aeroplanes	Barbers Tea	25
1956	Famous British Fliers	Turf Cigarettes	50
1956	Jet Aircraft of the World	R. L. Jones (drinks)	24
1957	Air Transport	Granose Foods	*16
1958	Aircraft of the World	Mills Cigarettes	25
1958	Modern Aircraft	Auto Machine Co	25
1958	British Aircraft	Clevedon Confectionery	50
1958	Aircraft of the World	Halpins Tea	25
1959	History of the Air (2 series)	Barratt & Co	48+25
1959	Aircraft of the World	Swettenham Tea	25
1961	Aircraft	B.T. Tea	25
1961	Wings Across the World	J. Lyons Products	24
1961	Aircraft	Priory Tea	50
1961	Landmarks of Flying	Sweetale Products	18
1962	Wings of Speed	J. Lyons Products	24
1962	Aircraft of World War II	Ringtons Tea	25
1963	Famous International Aircraft	Cleveton Confectionery	50
1963	International Air Liners	Glengettie Tea	25
1963	History of British Military Aircraft	Kellogg cereals	16
1963	History of Flight (2 series)	Rossi's Ice Cream	2×25
1964	History of Aviation	Bishop Stortford Dairy Farmers Tea	25
1966	Aircraft of World War II	Hitchman's Dairies	25
1970	International Air Liners	Polar Ice Cream	25
1973	History of Aviation	Brooke Bond Tea	50

*Larger than standard cards.

A number of the card sets had sticky backs for placing in albums. This trend started pre-war and has continued since. Sets, in or out of albums, and mixed lots, abound. Apart from dealers in cards whose names will be readily found in the *Exchange & Mart*, many antique and second-hand bookshops throughout the country sell cards in sets and mixed lots. The writer, wandering through Goathland on the North York moors as recently as August 1975, spotted packs of five cards for 2p on sale outside one of the two food shops in the village; on checking later it was found that some of these cards, sold at under ½p each, were valued at 40p each in a dealer's catalogues.

If you wish to combine a cartophilic interest with aviation, then the field is wide open; it is no more expensive than collecting books or model kits and the foregoing lists set a target — and you can always expand into other subjects. Moreover, the value of the collections will rise over the years.

Christmas cards

Aeronautica and Christmas may seem far removed, but the writer is one of many who have kept Christmas cards over the years that have a particular aeronautical interest.

Squadrons of the RFC, RNAS and RAF have had Christmas cards designed over the past 60-odd years, many bearing paintings, sketches or photographs by squadron members.

Between the wars, around September each year, squadrons and other units would decide on the design of their Christmas cards. Sometimes this took the form of the squadron's aircraft lined up on the ground or a photograph taken in the air in a squadron-run competition — the winner getting his cards free. Some of the results are in squadron albums today and others have been preserved by the recipients. Many of the beautiful photographs used in these cards have never been published. On the other hand, some squadrons wrote to aeronautical magazines with a request for permission to reproduce one of their photos, and so many a family of Christmas past had a Charles E. Brown photo among the snow scenes.

The aeronautical magazines are the recipients of hundreds of cards annually, and some have been preserved. Some January issues of *Flight* in the past, gave a full-page display of some of the magnificent cards they had received, most of which had an aeronautical theme. There are vintage years in aeronautical Christmas cards; 1918 the first RAF Christmas Card, 1943 and 1968 the main RAF anniversary years, 1975 the Royal Observer Corps 50th anniversary.

Whether cards have an aeronautical theme or not, a card signed by a famous ace like Albert Ball, or commander like Lord Trenchard or a record-breaker like Amy Johnson are now avidly sought and would be quite valuable. Truly, in the past much aeronautica has been discarded each year on the twelfth day of Christmas.

Propellers

Perhaps the most popular items of aeronautica are old wooden propellers. They symbolised the very power of an aircraft and their production was a work of craftsmanship. For strength it was important that there was cross-graining and most wooden propellers were made up of laminations of different woods. English ash, sycamore, walnut, grand bassam and Benin mahogany were among the many woods used in propeller manufacture, varnished for protection and finally polished. As a precaution against splintering some propellers were fabric covered and had brass sheaths fitted at the tips. Over 60 different firms in Britain and about the same number in Germany, produced wooden propellers 1914-1920. Some of the firms concerned were aircraft manufacturers, others specialist manufacturers. Their products were often marked with a transfer trade mark on each blade. As this was varnished over for protection even some of these trade marks have stood the test of time.

It is because the craftsmanship of an old propeller is aesthetically pleasing, that so many have been preserved. A census of extant 1914-1918 propellers could well run to four figures. They were sometimes salvaged as a memento of a crash and graves of airmen in France were often given a cross made from a propeller with the boss used for an etched plate. Propellers have adorned walls of messes at airfields and flying clubs. Many are held privately and others are stored away. Not only complete propellers, there are also many clocks presented to airmen, that have been set into a propeller boss with blades cropped. They adorn many a mantelpiece. Both complete and adapted propellers may be seen from time to time in antique shops.

A number of four-bladed propellers were used after World War 1 in table-making. It was a simple matter of adding a table top to two lopped four-bladers as illustrated. Usually the marked side was turned inward and the boss was given a wooden cap on the outside. A standard mahogany table top would make a good match for the blade legs. A five-seat form was once made of lopped propellers, but this was an exception.

Identifying propellers, World War 1

What every possessor of a propeller wants to know is its history. Each one made for British aircraft bore inspection and identification details. These can be interpreted to a degree. It should be appreciated that propellers were built for an engine to power a particular aircraft type, and that although there are fairly comprehensive records of the fitting of engines by maker's number and service number to aircraft by serial number, there are no records of the fitting of propellers to engines; it just is not now possible, in the normal course of research, to link a propeller with an individual aircraft. There may, of course, be exceptions where a propeller has been specially marked to show an association.

What propellers do normally show is their drawing number which can be indicative of the aircraft type for which they were designed. This, with other relevant information, is marked around the boss. In some cases markings were stamped, but to avoid splintering these were sometimes lightly burnt into the wood. These indications consisted of the propeller drawing number, rotation initials, diameter and pitch figures, for example: **LP 5300 RHT D2780 P2920** would stand for Lang Propeller to Drawing 5300, Right-Hand Tractor of diameter 2780 mm, and pitch 2920 mm. A letter suffix to the drawing number, when marked, indicated a subsequent modification in the propeller design. The prefix letters to the drawing number referred to design responsibility as follows: **A** Vickers Ltd. **AB** Air Board (later Air Ministry). **AD** Air Department (of the Admiralty). **AM** or **AMC** Aircraft Manufacturing Company (DH). **BA** Blackburn Aeroplane & Motor Company. **D** White and Thompson Ltd (later Norman Thompson). **FA** Fairey Aviation Company. **GW** Grahame White. **IPC** Integral Propeller

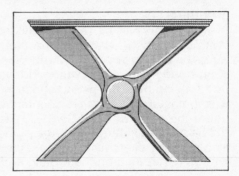

End view of table made from cropped props.

Company. **L** or **LP** Lang Propellers Ltd. **P** British & Colonial Aeroplane Co (Bristol). **S** Short Bros. **SC** United States Signal Corps. **T** Royal Aircraft Factory. **Y** A. V. Roe Ltd (Avro).

Propeller rotation initials related as follows: **LHP** Left-hand pusher. **LHT** Left-hand tractor. **RHP** Right-hand pusher. **RHT** Right-hand tractor.

At the end of World War 1, a standard register of propeller types was compiled and a standard system of identification introduced. This three-figure system consisted of three parts, marked on each propeller as follows: Drawing number (prefix letter/letters identified manufacturing firm as given above); Group number (prefixed by G); Serial number (prefixed by N).

Up to the early 1920s 'propeller' was the accepted term, but it was then changed to 'airscrew' in official parlance until the late 1930s when 'propeller' once again became the accepted term.

Clock stand prop bosses fetch only a few pounds, but complete wooden propellers from World War 1 aircraft now fetch from £25 upwards. The applicability of propellers, by drawing numbers, is given in Appendix B.

Designations, World War 2

The sophisticated propellers of World War 2 with variable pitch and constant speed units had a far more complicated system of designations and each company used their own system. Rotol, the more widely used, had indicative figures and letters. To give as an example the R12/4F5/2 propeller fitted to Spitfire Mks VIII & IX: R = Rotol Ltd (the manufacturer), 12 = 12th type in 4F5 series, 4 = four-bladed, F = fighter aircraft, 5 = No 5 size shaft, 2 = 2nd modification of basic design. Rotol also used prefix letters RX to denote hydraulic non-standard, RS for hydraulic standard and RE for electric.

American propellers bore reference numbers indicative of the type for which they were designed, as listed in Appendix C.

Aviation art and drawings

In spite of a welter of art books in general, there are few devoted to aircraft subjects. This is not because aviation has yet to acquire the veneration due to age, for among the popular art reproductions in the high street shops and shopping centres are reproductions of many contemporary artists such as Peter Scott and Vernon Ward bird studies, and Rowland Hilder landscapes — but few are of air studies.

The masters

Aviation art can be roughly divided into sections. Firstly, and perhaps foremost, are the works of the masters in aviation art, such as Joseph Simpson of World War 1, Frank Wootten's paintings of World War 2 and John Young's in recent years. The value of some of these paintings runs into four figures. Simpson, whose works are held by some RAF stations, was a master of detail. He accompanied Captain Ewart, RFA, who wrote under the name of Boyd Cable, to France in 1918 as a war artist. Not only did he discuss settings with the airmen concerned, and get their approval to his rough sketches, but he sketched with matched colours with the aircraft concerned on the airfield and examined captured German aircraft to present both friend and foe in authentic colours. Due to the restricted display of Simpson's pictures his work has never received the acclaim that it deserves.

Famous as a war artist, Frank Wootten has achieved further fame in other fields. From a letter that appeared in *Flight International* in 1976 it appears that the artist himself is not sure of the present whereabouts of all his pictures and so it is possible that some of his aeronautical works have yet to come to light. Frank Wootten is currently honorary president of the Guild of Aviation Artists which has done much to promote aviation art. Exhibitions are held annually and are notified in advance in *Flight International's* aviation calendar. Many of the pictures displayed are for sale and here is the opportunity to view with a view to buying an item that catches the eye, or to indulge in the appreciation of aviation art.

The guild is, strictly speaking, a body of aeronautical artists since lighter-than-air subjects are included in their scope. Formed in 1971, it is a guild of professional and non-professional painters interested in promoting aviation art by the organisation of exhibitions, exchange of ideas and techniques through meetings, lectures and newsletters. Enquiries for membership should be addressed to The Secretary (Mrs Yvonne Bonham), The Guild of Aviation Artists, 11 Great Spilmans, London SE22 SZL.

Unfortunately exhibitions are limited largely to London and since many of the best paintings are in private houses, RAF messes and aeronautical clubs, they are only seen by a privileged few. Not so the works of the cover artists.

Much expertise is displayed by the commercial artists. Roy Cross, both author and artist and now an accomplished marine artist, is the artist responsible for many of the Airfix model boxes and cover paintings of the PSL Classic Aircraft series among others, so his art is probably the most frequently seen. Unfortunately, titling and details spoil many of the paintings and so few collect model boxes on that score. But some book covers have become collectors' items.

The Harleyford series of books, which were in a consistent size and presentation style, used the talented and painstaking artist Douglas Carrick. So well received were his paintings that there was a separate demand for frontispiece reproductions from the book and this led to a special series of large poster-like reproductions of his work. Several firms in Britain and America now market poster and aviation art studies. These are not so much collectors' items, as the object of large reproductions is wall display, and space is a limiting factor. In this field the collector is usually looking for a small number of reproductions for room or house decoration, preferably in a uniform size and styling.

Trends change, while the appreciation of graphic art is unchanged over the years, buyers are now much more insistent upon accuracy. One well-known artist, commissioned by a very famous magazine, had a most appalling eye for aircraft shapes, and while this did not matter at the time when the aircraft were rather remote from the readership, the originals of his work are now practically worthless.

The master of graphic cover art was undoubtedly S. Drigin who painted over 50 covers in bright colours for the pulp magazine *Air Stories.* Such was their appeal, that when the magazines were discarded, the covers were often kept and collected. Graphic art is sometimes used today to make a magazine stand out from others, but while such covers are more arresting, they lack the appeal of a Drigin.

A post-war trend is the commissioning of artists to portray an aircraft type flown or owned. This may be on a canvas in a setting, or a profile view where draughtsmanship counts in accurately detailing the aircraft and its markings. The usual fee is around £20 for single profile view.

The modelling market has led from aircraft general arrangement views in tones, to full-colour illustrations. These reached a high standard in the Profile Publications of aircraft studies under the editorship of Charles W. Cain and a particularly high standard is evident in Pilot Press and some Ducimus publications. In this field, names like P. Endsleigh Castle and James Goulding have come to the fore and altogether, while the Profile series lasted, a dozen different artists were used with very little to choose between them in the excellent execution of their work. The original artwork, which is usually done on white surfaced hardboard, would make excellent display material, particularly the profile views, and could become collectors' items.

Plans

The origins of aircraft plan collecting go back to the days before modelling was merely the assembling of plastic moulds, but whittling into shape blocks, sheets and strips of balsa wood. Wings and fuselage were shaped by hand and accurate drawings were necessary, the popular scale being 1:72nd. The *Aeromodeller* featured plans and started a plans service which has been flourishing for some 30 years. Catalogues are available and enquiries on individual aircraft plans can be made, if accompanied by stamped addressed envelope, to Model & Allied Press (Plans Service), PO Box 35, Hemel Hempstead, Herts HP1 1EE.

A feature of most of the Harleyford books was 1:72nd scale general arrangement drawings, involving folded pages to accommodate the large flying boats at this scale of *Marine Aircraft of the 1914-1918 War*. One of the best books of plans of obscure aircraft types in recent years has been *The Aircraft of the Swiss Air Force since 1914* published in 1975 by Verlag Th Gut, which had some 175 full page (10 × 8 inch) three-view general arrangement drawings. Hopefully, it will be reprinted.

The most fruitful sources of GA scale drawings are the various aeronautical magazines produced over the past 60 years.

Models

While few people are fortunate enough to be able to afford a full-size aeroplane, collecting models of favourite types is well within the capabilities of the youngest schoolboy. Plastic construction kits of literally hundreds of types are now available in a variety of scales from American, British, Japanese, German, Italian and other international manufacturers, and if assembled with care and patience can form most attractive display and conversation pieces. While at first sight their value as collectors' items may seem limited, a brief review of the actual situation shows that this is far from the truth, for manufacturers are constantly dropping their earlier or less successful lines from their catalogues, and many of these acquire high values. Even kits which were widely available a mere five or six years ago and have since disappeared are now eagerly sought by modellers wishing to add unusual types to their collections, while the early Skybirds and Frog Penguin models from the 1930s and '40s can today fetch £25 or more apiece.

It is difficult to predict from current ranges which models will become tomorrow's collectors' items, since many models which one would never dream would be dropped, are (such as the Frog trio of V-bombers which are among the most sought-after kits even though they were only abandoned some ten years or so ago); while others for which one can see no ready market apparently still sell and sell. Good prospects for stashing away are kits of prototype or experimental aircraft which never in fact got into mass production, such as the Airfix Saunders Roe SR53; and early models from any of the manufacturers' ranges, since in due course these will probably be discarded and re-introduced as brand new, re-tooled kits. Occasionally a manufacturer cheats, and re-introduces an old kit in virtually the same form except for new box artwork, so you can't always strike lucky, but many collectors value the old boxes and instruction sheets as highly as the kits themselves. Another possibility is the various ranges of vacuum-moulded kits which are produced in limited runs by enterprising private manufacturers, and are rarely re-marketed once the initial production batch has been sold.

The future

We have been looking at the past and the items once commonplace that have become valuable; but what of the commonplace items of today that in years to come will be valuable? It would be difficult to predict for in the past we discarded much that might have been of value and the range is wide. The writer's prediction is that books and magazines will provide the best investment. Even if books are remaindered at the time, this does mean that they are out of print and may well be sought later. With magazines, once published they are hardly ever reprinted and complete mint sets often command good prices after a few years. Moreover, due to holidays and other preoccupations, a particular issue may not be given the attention it deserved. When copies are kept as an investment they are always available for perusal.

Aeronautical museums now abound and a new trend is now evident to contest with the rather static nature of the majority of exhibits, making use of sound recording and video tape. While film projected on to the domed cover creates the illusion of sky and the sounds suggest your engine is being run up, you mount a Link trainer type of structure, enter the cockpit set out like a fighter, and as you move the control column about you — dammit — aeronautica was meant to be a form of escapism from rock and roll!

Appendix A

WORLD WAR 1 AIRFIELDS AND BASES

Aldeburgh, Suffolk (Marine Observers Flying School)
Aldergrove, Belfast (No 16 AAP near eastern shore of Loch Neagh)
All Hallows, Kent (LG)
Andover, Hants (navigation and bombing school)
Anglesea (Llangefni), Wales (airship station)
Anwick, Lincs (LG)
Appleton Wiske, Yorks (LG)
Arlington, Sussex (LG)
Ashington, Northumberland (aerodrome)
Atwick Racecourse, Hull (LG)
Auldbar, Forfar (airship sub-station)
Ayr, Scotland (School of Aerial Fighting)
Bacton, Norfolk (night LG)
Baldonnel, Ireland (No 23 TDS)
Ballycastle, Co Antrim (aerodrome)
Ballywater, Co Down (aerodrome)
Bangor, Caernarvon (aerodrome for DH6s)
Barlow, Selby Yorks (Armstrong Whitworth airship construction)
Barmby, Yorks (LG)
Barrow-in-Furness (airship station)
Beaulieu, Hants (No 29 TDS)
Bedford (Cardington airship construction station)
Bekesbourne, near Canterbury (aerodrome)
Bellasize, Yorks(LG)
Bembridge, IoW (SP station, see also New Bembridge)
Benton, Northumberland (LG)
Berehaven, Ireland (US Navy balloon base)
Beverley, Yorks (aerodrome)
Bicester, Oxford (aerodrome)
Biggin Hill, Kent (aerodrome)
Binsoe, Yorks (LG)
Bircham Newton, Norfolk (aerodrome)

Bishopton, Durham (LG)
Blackheath, Chelmsford (LG)
Bognor, Sussex (Norman Thompson SP works)
Boscombe Down, Wilts (No 6 TDS)
Bournemouth (Winton Aerodrome)
Bowness-in-Windemere (private SP school)
Bracebridge, Lincs (AAP)
Braham Moor, see Tadcaster
Brancroft, Yorks (LG)
Brattleby (see Scampton)
Brigmerston Down (LG)
Brockworth, Glos (factory airfield)
Brooklands, Surrey (racetrack centre used as testing airfield by several manufacturers and No 10 AAP)
Broomfield, near Chelmsford (LG)
Broomfield, Herne Bay (LG)
Brough, Yorks (factory airfield)
Buckminster, near Grantham (AAP not completed)
Bucknell, Salop (LG)
Bude, Cornwall (airship sub-station)
Burgh Castle, Suffolk (night LG)
Burnham-on-Crouch, Essex (LG)
Bury (Ramsey), Hunts (airfield became Upwood)
Butley, Sussex (experimental flying station)
Cairncross, Berwick (LG)
Caldale, Orkneys (balloon base)
Calshot, Hants (SP base)
Capel, Kent (airship station)
Cardington (see Bedford)
Carlton, Yorks (LG)
Castlebar, Ireland (aerodrome)
Castle Bromwich (TDS, later AAP)
Castle Donington, Derby (LG)
Catfirth, Shetlands (seaplane station)
Cathcart, Glasgow (factory airfield)
Catterick, Yorks (No 49 TDS)
Cattewater, Plymouth (seaplane base, became Mount Batten)

Chathill, Holy Island (airship sub-station)

Chattis Hill, Wilts (No 43 TDS)

Chickerill, Dorset (aerodrome)

Chiddingstone Causeway, Kent (LG)

Chingford, Essex (aerodrome)

Coal Aston, Sheffield (No 2 ARD)

Collinstown, Ireland (No 24 TDS)

Cookstown (renamed Tallaght)

Copmanthorpe, Yorks (aerodrome)

Cottenham, Cambs (LG)

Covehithe, Norfolk (night LG)

Coventry (No 1 AAP)

Cowes, IoW (factory and service airfield)

Crail, Fife (No 27 TDS)

Cramlington, Northumberland (No 52 TDS)

Cranmore, near Galway (aerodrome)

Cranwell, Lincs (airship base, three TDSs, North and South airfields)

Cricklewood, London (factory airfield)

Croydon, Surrey (aerodrome)

Cullercoats, Northumberland (LG)

Currugh, Ireland (aerodrome)

Dalmuir, Dumbarton (factory airfield)

Detling, Kent (aerodrome)

Didsbury, Manchester (AAP under construction)

Doncaster, Yorks (No 47 TDS)

Donibristle, Fifeshire (Fleet aircraft base)

Dover, Kent (Swingate Downs, Guston Road naval aerodrome and East Pier SP station)

Driffield, Yorks (No 21 TDS)

Dundee, Angus (SP station)

Dunkeswicke, Yorks (LG)

Duxford, Cambs (No 35 TDS)

Earls Farm Down, Hants (LG)

Earnley, Sussex (LG)

Earsham, Norfolk (LG)

Easington, York (LG)

Eastbourne, Sussex (No 50 TDS)

Eastburn, became Driffield

Eastchurch, Kent (No 204 TDS and experimental station)

East Fortune, E. Lothian (aerodrome and airship station)

Eastleigh, Hants (US Navy air station and AAP)

Easton-on-Hill, Northants (No 5 TDS)

East Retford, Notts (aerodrome)

Edzell, Brechin (No 26 TDS)

Elsham, Lindsay, Lincs (LG)

Elmswell, Suffolk (LG)

Fairlop, Essex (No 54 TDS)

Farnborough, Hants (depot, construction, No 1 ARD and experimental work; railway access)

Felixstowe, Suffolk (flying boat base)

Feltham, Middx (factory airfield)

Feltham reservoir, Middx (aerial firing site)

Feltwell, Norfolk (No 7 TDS)

Filton, near Bristol (service aerodrome and factory airfield)

Fishguard, Pembroke (SP station)

Flower Down, near Winchester (Wireless School)

Ford Farm (became Old Sarum)

Ford Junction, Sussex (US Air Service and RAF station)

Fowlmere, Cambs (No 31 TDS. Note, on different site than World War 2 Fowlmere satellite)

Freethorpe, Norfolk (LG)

Freiston, Lincs (No 4 Fighting School)

Frinstead, Kent (LG)

Fyfield, Essex (LG)

Gifford, East Lothian (LG)

Gilling, Yorks (LG)

Gilmerton, Edinburgh (LG)

Godmersham Park, Kent (airship sub-station)

Goldhanger, Essex (LG)

Gormanston, Ireland (No 22 TDS)

Gosberton, Lincs (LG)

Gosport, Hants (SP Base)

Grain, Isle of (Naval air experimental station factory airfield)

Greenland Top, Yorks (LG)

Grimista, Lerwick (balloon base)

Grimsthorpe Park, Lincs (bombing ground)

Grove Park, Kent (LG and RAF MT depot)

Gullane, Firth of Forth (No 2 TDS)

Hainault Farm, Ilford (aerodrome)

Halfpenny House Moor, Yorks (bombing ground)

Halton, Bucks (Australian Flying Corps, Wendover airfield)

Hamble, Hants (factory field and SP slipways)

Harwick, Cambs (private training school)

Harlaxton, Lincs (No 40 TDS)

Harpswell (see Hemswell)

Harling Road, Norfolk (aerodrome)

Harty, Kent (LG)

Hawkinge, Kent (No 12 AAP)

Hayes, Middx (factory airfield)
Hedon, Yorks (LG)
Helperby, Yorks (aerodrome)
Hemswell, Lincs (Harpswell aerodrome)
Hendon, London (No 2 AAP and factory fields)
Henlow, Beds (No 5 ARD)
Hickling Broad, Norfolk (SP sub-station)
Hippenscombe, Hants (bombing ground)
Holt, Norfolk (night LG)
Hooten Park, Cheshire (No 4 TDS)
Hornsea, Yorks (SP station)
Horsegate, Durham (LG)
Horseheath, Cambs (LG)
Hounslow, Middx (No 42 TDS)
Houten Bay, near Kirkwall (flying boat station)
Howden, Yorks (airship station)
Hucknall, Notts (No 15 TDS)
Hylton (renamed Usworth July 15 1918)
Hythe, Kent (School of Gunnery)
Inchinnan, Glasgow (airship station and aerodrome)
Immingham, Lincs (airship construction)
Joyce Green, near Dartford (aerodrome)
Kelstern, Lincs (LG)
Kenley, Surrey (No 7 AAP)
Kettleness, Yorks (Naval LG)
Kilconquhar, Fife (LG)
Killingholme, Lincs (SP base and aerodrome, RAF/US Navy)
Kingshill, Kent (LG)
Kingsnorth, Kent (airship base)
Kirkleatham, Yorks (airship sub-station)
Kirton Lindsay, Lincs (aerodrome)
Knavesmire, York Racecourse (LG)
Laira, Plymouth (airship sub-station)
Lakenheath, Suffolk (bombing ground)
Lake Down, Salisbury (aerodrome)
Larkhill, Wilts (No 1 Balloon School and aerodrome)
Larne, Ireland (airship portable shed)
Leadenham, Lincs (aerodrome)
Leagrave, Beds (factory airfield)
Lee-on-Solent, Hants (SP base)
Leigherton, Glos (aerodrome)
Leuchars, Fife (fleet aircraft base)
Leysdown, Kent (aerodrome)
Lilbourne, Northants (aerodrome)
Lincoln (No 4 AAP)
Little Downham (LG)
Loch Doon (School of Gunnery abandoned)

London Colney, Herts (No 41 TDS)
Longhorsley, Northumberland (LG)
Longside, Aberdeen (airship station and aerodrome)
Lopcombe Corner, Wilts (No 3 TDS)
Lower Beeding, Sussex (LG)
Lowestoft, Suffolk (seaplane and balloon base)
Lowthorpe, near Bridlington (airship mooring and LG)
Luce Bay, Wigtown (airship station)
Lydd, Kent (No 2 Balloon School)
Lyme Regis (renamed Toller May 2 1918)
Lympne, Kent (No 8 AAP)
Malahide, Dublin (airship sub-station)
Manston, Kent (aerodrome)
Manywell Heights, Yorks (LG)
Marden, Kent (LG)
Marham, Norfolk (aerodrome)
Market Deeping, Lincs (LG)
Marske, Yorks (School of Aerial Fighting & Gunnery)
Manchester (No 15 AAP Alexandra Park)
Martlesham Heath, Suffolk (Aeroplane Experimental Station)
Menthorpe Gate, Yorks (LG)
Meriden, Warwick (LG)
Merifield, Tor Point, Cornwall (No 16 Balloon Base)
Milford Haven (No 9 Balloon Base)
Minchinhampton, Glos (aerodrome)
Montrose, Forfar (No 32 TDS)
Mullion, Cornwall (airship shed and airfield)
Murton, Durham (LG)
Narborough, Norfolk (aerodrome)
Netheravon, Wilts (Nos 8 and 12 TDSs)
Newcastle (Town Moor Aerodrome, 9 AAP)
New Bembridge, IoW (aerodrome)
New Chapel, Surrey (LG)
New Haggerston, Berwick (aerodrome)
Newhaven, Sussex (SP station)
New Holland, Yorks (LG)
Newlyn, Cornwall (SP station)
North Benfleet, Essex (LG)
North Coates Fitties, Lincs (aerodrome)
North Queensferry (No 18 Balloon Base)
Norwich (factory fields)
Northolt, Middx (No 30 TDS)
North Weald Basset (aerodrome)
Novar (became Evanton, 1936)
Old Sarum, Salisbury (No 11 TDS)
Old Weston, Thrapston

Omagh, Tyrone (aerodrome)

Orfordness, Suffolk (armament experimental station)

Orsett, Essex (LG)

Owthorne, near Withernsea (LG)

Orton, Westmorland (LG)

Padstow, Cornwall (aerodrome)

Palmers Farm, Essex (LG)

Pembroke (airship base and aerodrome)

Penshurst, Kent (aerodrome)

Penston, E. Lothian (aerodrome)

Pentridge, Hants (LG)

Peterhead, Aberdeen (SP station)

Pluckley, Kent (LG)

Plungar, Notts (LG)

Polegate, near Eastbourne (airship station)

Pontefract, Yorks (LG)

Ponteland, Northumberland (LG)

Portholme Meadow, Hunts (aerodrome)

Portland, Dorset (seaplane base)

Port Meadow, Oxford (No 44 TDS)

Port Mellon, Scillies (flying boat moorings)

Prawle, Devon (aerodrome)

Pulham, Norfolk (airship experimental station)

Queniborough Leics (LG)

Rathmullan, Lough Swilly (No 13 Balloon Base)

Redcar, Yorks (No 2 School of Special Flying)

Rendcombe, Cirencester (No 45 TDS)

Renfrew, Glasgow (ARD under construction)

Richmond Park, Surrey (Balloon Training Depot. Sites at Kingston Hill and Beverley Brook)

Ripon Racecourse (LG)

Rochester, Kent (factory, SP slipways, etc)

Rochford, Essex (aerodrome site of Southend Airport)

Rollestone Camp (see Larkhill)

Rosyth, Fife (SP depot)

Rye, Sussex (LG)

Sadberge, Durham (LG)

Sawbridgeworth, Hants (LG)

Saxthorpe, Norfolk (LG)

Scalby Mills, Scarborough (SP sub-station)

Scale Hall, Lancs (LG)

Scampton, Lincs (No 34 TDS)

Scapa (balloon base and aircraft repair depot)

Scopwick, Lincs (aerodrome, renamed Digby in 1922)

Seacroft, near Leeds (LG)

Sea Houses, Northumberland (aerodrome)

Seaton Carew, Durham (aerodrome and SP station)

Sedgeford, Norfolk (No 3 Fighting School)

Shawbury, Salop (No 9 TDS)

Sheerness, Kent (balloon base and LG)

Sherburn-in-Elmet, Yorks (AAP)

Shotley, Harwich (No 12 Balloon Base)

Shoreham, Sussex (aerodrome)

Shotwick, Cheshire (No 51 TDS aerodrome, became Sealand 1924)

Shrewsbury (AAP not completed)

Sible Hedingham, Essex (LG)

Slindon, Sussex (airship sub-station)

Smethwick, Worcs (aerodrome)

Smoogroo, Orkneys (aerodrome for Fleet practice)

Sole Street, Kent (LG)

South Ash, Kent (LG)

South Carlton, Lincs (No 46 TDS)

South Cave, Yorks (LG)

South Denes, Yarmouth (aerodrome)

South Farnborough (see Farnborough)

South Otterington, Yorks (LG)

Southport, Lancs (aerodrome on sands)

Stonehenge, Wilts (aerodrome)

South Shields (SP base and Marine Aircraft Depot)

Spennymore, Durham (LG)

Spitalgate, Lincs (aerodrome, later became Grantham)

Sporle, Norfolk (LG)

Stag Lane, Edgeware (factory airfield)

Stallingborough, Lincs (LG)

Stamford, Lincs (renamed Wittering April 10 1918)

Stanstead, Herts (St Margaret's Night LG two miles SE of Ware)

Stenness, Orkneys (SP station)

Stow Maries, Essex (aerodrome)

Strathbeg (SP station)

Sutton's Farm (aerodrome, became Hornchurch)

Swingfield, near Dover (LG)

Swingate Downs (see Dover)

Tadcaster, Yorks (No 38 TDS)

Tallaght, Ireland (No 25 TDS)

Tangmere, Sussex (No 61 TDS)

Telscombe, Cliffs, Sussex (aerodrome)

Ternhill, Salop (aerodrome)

Thaxted, Essex (LG)

Therfield, Baldock (HD airfield)
Thetford, Norfolk (No 4 School of Navigation and Bomb Dropping)
Thornaby, Yorks (LG)
Thorne, Yorks (LG)
Throwley, Faversham (HD airfield)
Thurgarton, Notts (LG)
Tibenham, Norfolk (LG)
Tipnor, Portsmouth (No 15 Balloon Base)
Toller, Dorset (airship sub-station)
Torquay, Devon (SP station)
Trescoe, Scillies (flying boat station)
Turnberry, near Givan (aerodrome)
Turnhouse, Edinburgh (HD airfield and Fleet Practice Ground)
Tydd St Mary, near Wisbech (LG)
Tynehead, Midlothian (LG)
Tynemouth (aerodrome)
Upavon, Wilts (aerodrome)
Upper Heyford, Oxford (aerodrome)
Upton, Poole (airship sub-station)
Usworth, Durham (No 36 TDS)
Waddington, Lincs (No 48 TDS)
Walmer, Kent (aerodrome)
Ware, Herts (LG relinquished mid-1918 in favour of Stanstead)
Wash, The (area used as bombing range)
Waterloo Sands, Lancs (LG)
West Ayton, Scarborough (aerodrome)
West Fenton (renamed Gullane April 17 1918)
Westgate, Kent (SP station and aerodrome)

West Malling (see Kingshill)
Weston-on-the-Green, Bicester (No 28 TDS)
Westpole Farm, Essex (LG)
Westward Ho, Devon (aerodrome)
Wexford (Johnstone Castle airship sub-station also used by US Navy)
Weybridge, Surrey (Vickers airfield)
Whiteburn, Grant's House
Wight, Cowes (aerodrome)
Wigsley, Notts (LG)
Willian, Herts (LG)
Wilsford Down, Wilts (bombing ground)
Wimbledon, London (night LG)
Wingates Moor, Northumberland (bombing ground)
Winterton, Yorks (LG)
Winton (see Bournemouth)
Witney, Oxford (No 33 TDS)
Wittering, Northants (aerodrome)
Wormingford, Essex (LG)
Wormwood Scrubs, London (airship construction)
Wye, Kent (aerodrome)
Wyton, Hunts (aerodrome)
Yapton (renamed Ford)
Yarmouth, Norfolk (seaplane base and aerodrome)
Yarnbury Castle, Wilts (bombing ground)
Yate, Bristol (No 3 ARD)
Yatesbury, Wilts (Eastern & Western aerodromes)
Yelling, St Neots (HD airfield)
Yeovil, Somerset (Westland airfield)

Appendix B

WORLD WAR 2
AIRFIELD LOCATION MAPS

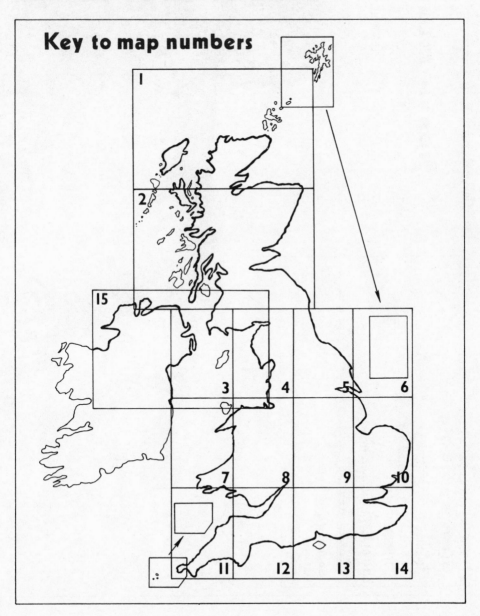

Key to map numbers

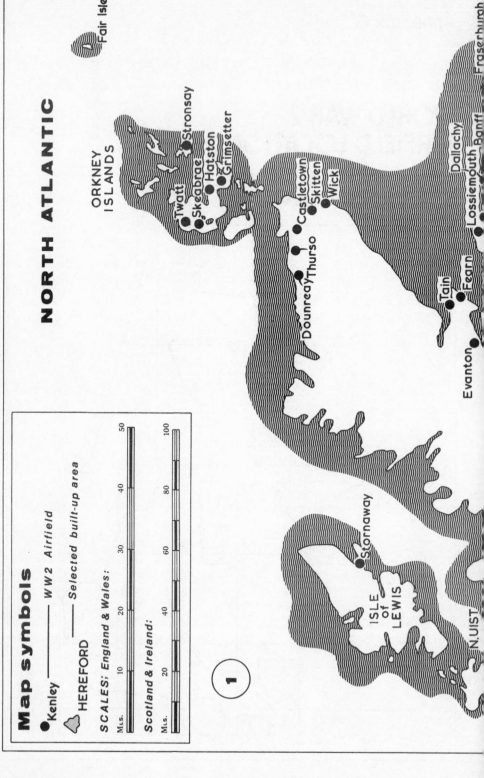

NORTH ATLANTIC

Fair Isle

ORKNEY
ISLANDS

Stronsay
Skeabrae
Twatt
Hatston
Grimsetter

Castletown
Skitten
Wick
Dounreay
Thurso

Dallachy
Lossiemouth
Banff
Fraserburgh

Tain
Fearn
Evanton

Stornaway

ISLE
of
LEWIS

N.UIST

Map symbols

● Kenley — WW2 Airfield

▲ HEREFORD — Selected built-up area

SCALES: England & Wales:

Mls. | 10 | 20 | 30 | 40 | 50

Scotland & Ireland:

Mls. | 20 | 40 | 60 | 80 | 100

1

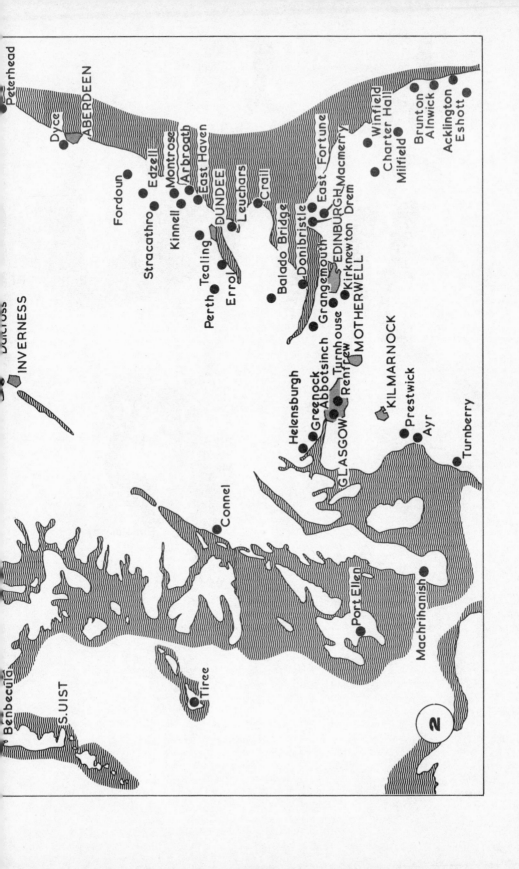

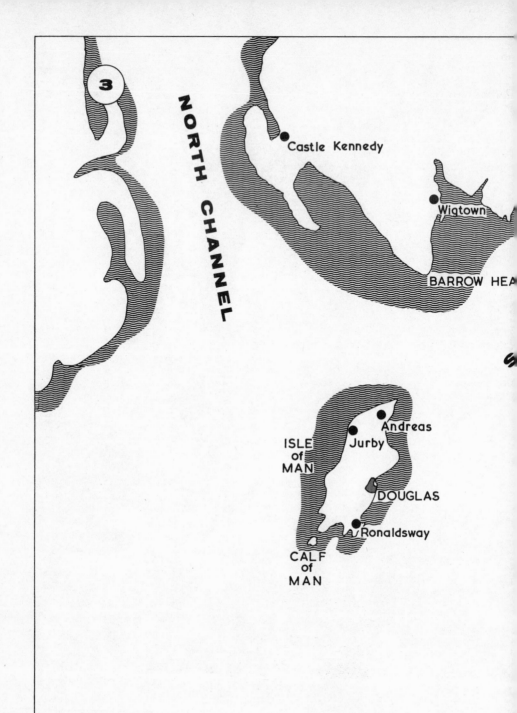

3

NORTH CHANNEL

● Castle Kennedy

● Wigtown

BARROW HEA

ISLE
of
MAN

● Andreas
● Jurby

DOUGLAS

● Ronaldsway

CALF
of
MAN

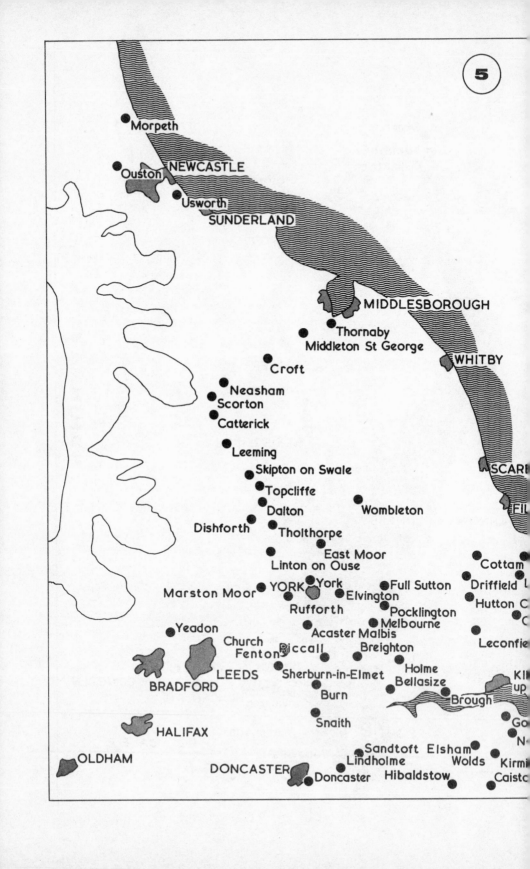

6

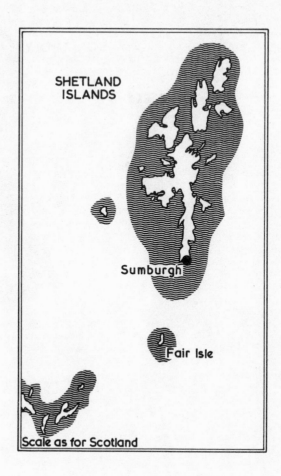

SHETLAND
ISLANDS

Sumburgh

Fair Isle

Scale as for Scotland

UGH

AMBOROUGH
HEAD

aby

ick

s

ON
LL

WITHERNSEA

illingholme

GRIMSBY

Grimsby

North Coates

NORTH
SEA

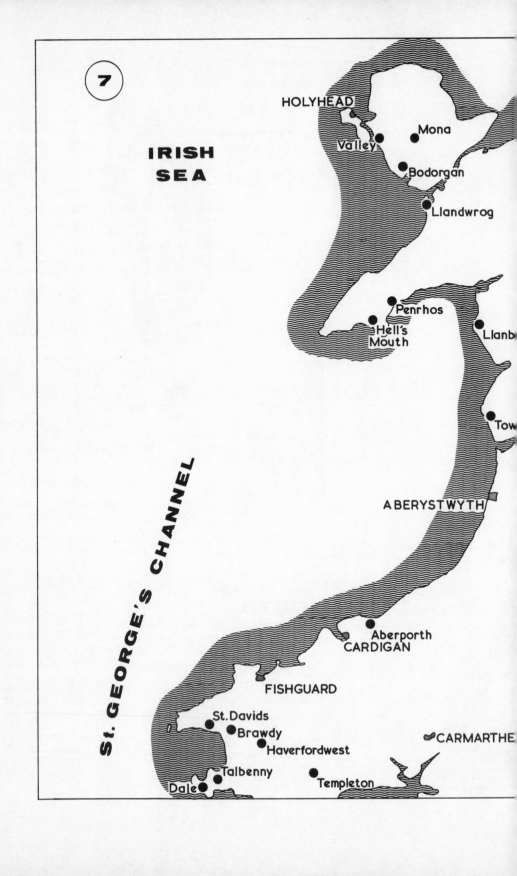

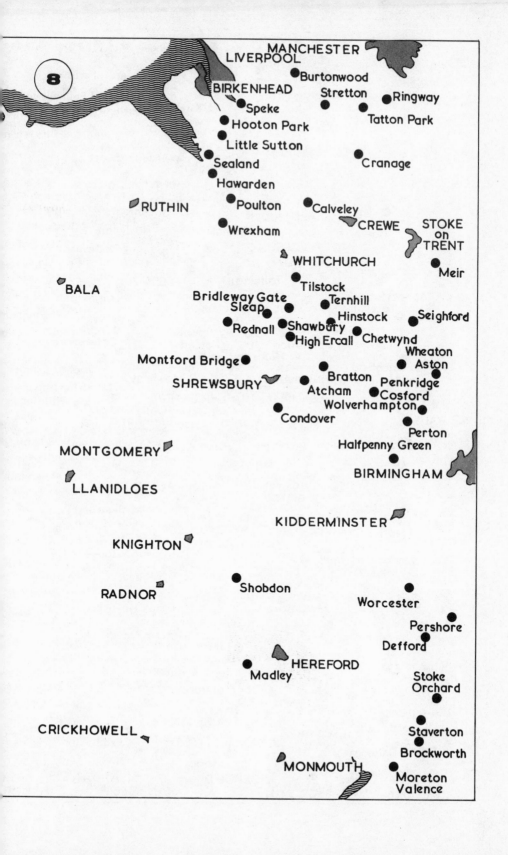

MANCHESTER
LIVERPOOL
Burtonwood
BIRKENHEAD
Stretton
Ringway
Speke
Tatton Park
Hooton Park
Little Sutton
Sealand
Cranage
Hawarden
RUTHIN
Poulton
Calveley
CREWE
Wrexham
STOKE
on
TRENT
Meir
WHITCHURCH
BALA
Tilstock
Bridleway Gate
Ternhill
Sleap
Hinstock
Seighford
Rednall
Shawbury
Chetwynd
High Ercall
Wheaton
Montford Bridge
Aston
Bratton
Penkridge
SHREWSBURY
Atcham
Cosford
Wolverhampton
Condover
Perton
Halfpenny Green
MONTGOMERY
LLANIDLOES
BIRMINGHAM
KIDDERMINSTER
KNIGHTON
RADNOR
Shobdon
Worcester
Pershore
Defford
HEREFORD
Madley
Stoke
Orchard
CRICKHOWELL
Staverton
Brockworth
MONMOUTH
Moreton
Valence

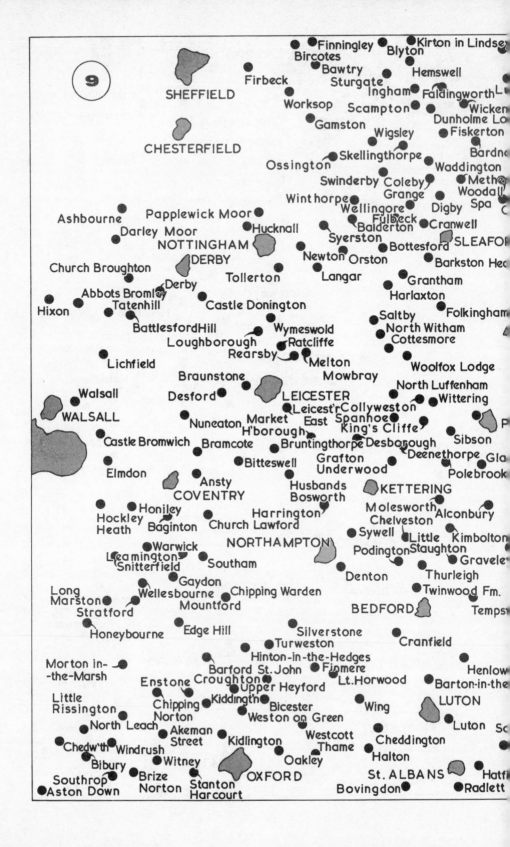

9

Finningley • • Kirton in Lindse
• • Blyton
Bircotes
Bawtry • Hemswell
SHEFFIELD Firbeck • Sturgate
• Ingham • Faldingworth L
Worksop • Scampton • Wicken
Dunholme Lo
Gamston • Wigsley • Fiskerton
CHESTERFIELD
Skellingthorpe • Bardn
Ossington • • Waddington
Swinderby Coleby • Methe
Grange • Woodall
Winthorpe • Digby Spa
Ashbourne Papplewick Moor • Wellingore •
Darley Moor • Hucknall Fulbeck • Cranwell
Balderton
NOTTINGHAM • Syerston • SLEAFO
DERBY Newton Orston • Bottesford
Tollerton • Barkston Hea
Derby Langar • Grantham
Abbots Bromley Harlaxton
Tatenhill Castle Donington Saltby Folkingham
Hixon • North Witham
BattlesfordHill Wymeswold Cottesmore
Loughborough Ratcliffe
Rearsby Melton Woolfox Lodge
Lichfield Mowbray
Braunstone North Luffenham
Walsall Desford LEICESTER Wittering
WALSALL Leicest'r Collyweston
Nuneaton Market East Spanhoe
H'borough King's Cliffe
Castle Bromwich Bramcote Bruntingthorpe Desborough Sibson
Bitteswell Grafton Deenethorpe Gla
Elmdon Underwood Polebrook
Ansty Husbands KETTERING
COVENTRY Bosworth
Honiley Harrington Molesworth Alconbury
Hockley Baginton Church Lawford Chelveston
Heath Sywell Little Kimbolton
Warwick Podington Staughton
Leamington NORTHAMPTON Gravele
Snitterfield Southam Thurleigh
Gaydon Denton Twinwood Fm.
Long Wellesbourne Chipping Warden
Marston Mountford BEDFORD Temps
Stratford Edge Hill Silverstone Cranfield
Honeybourne Turweston
Hinton-in-the-Hedges
Morton in- Barford St.John Finmere Henlow
-the-Marsh Enstone Croughton Lt.Horwood Barton-in-the
Upper Heyford
Little Chipping Kiddingt'n Bicester Wing LUTON
Rissington Norton Weston on Green
North Leach Akeman Westcott Cheddington Luton S
Street Kidlington Thame
Chedw'th Windrush Oakley Halton
Bibury Witney
Southrop Brize OXFORD St. ALBANS Hatfi
Aston Down Norton Stanton Bovingdon Radlett
Harcourt

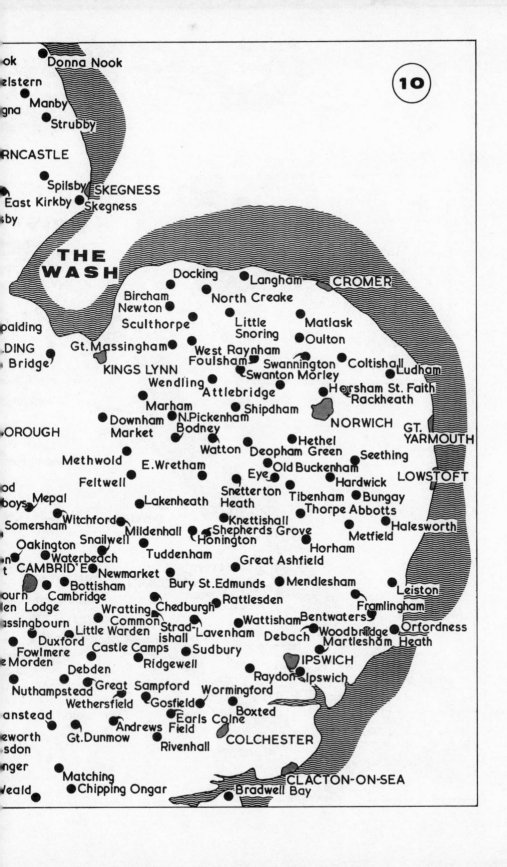

ok
Donna Nook
elstern
gna
Manby
Strubby
RNCASTLE

Spilsby SKEGNESS
East Kirkby Skegness
by

THE
WASH

palding
DING
Bridge

Docking
Langham CROMER
North Creake
Bircham
Newton
Sculthorpe
Little
Snoring
Matlask
Oulton
Gt. Massingham
West Raynham
Foulsham
Swannington Coltishall
KINGS LYNN
Swanton Morley Ludham
Wendling
Attlebridge
Horsham St. Faith
Rackheath
Marham
Shipdham
Downham N. Pickenham
Market Bodney
NORWICH GT.
YARMOUTH
OROUGH
Watton Deopham Green
Hethel
Seething
Methwold E. Wretham
Eye Old Buckenham
LOWSTOFT
Feltwell
Hardwick
od Snetterton
boys Mepal Lakenheath Heath Tibenham Bungay
Somersham Witchford Thorpe Abbotts
Knettishall Metfield Halesworth
Oakington Snailwell Mildenhall Shepherds Grove
Honington
Waterbeach Tuddenham Horham
CAMBRID'E Newmarket Great Ashfield
Bottisham Bury St.Edmunds Mendlesham
ourn Cambridge Leiston
en Lodge Wratting Rattlesden
ssingbourn Common Chedburgh Framlingham
Little Warden Strad- Wattisham Bentwaters
Duxford ishall Lavenham Debach Woodbridge Orfordness
Fowlmere Castle Camps Martlesham Heath
Morden Sudbury
Debden Ridgewell IPSWICH
Raydon Ipswich
Nuthampstead Great Sampford Wormingford
Wethersfield Gosfield Boxted
anstead Earls Colne
eworth Andrews Field COLCHESTER
sdon Gt.Dunmow
nger Rivenhall
CLACTON-ON-SEA
Matching
Weald Chipping Ongar Bradwell Bay

10

Angle

Carew Cheriton

Manorbier

Pembrey

Fairwood
Common

BRISTO

ISLES
of
SCILLY

PE

St. Mary's

Chiver

BIDEFC

GT. TORRING

Winkleigh

Cleave

BUDE

Okehampton

Davidstow
Moor

LAUNCESTON

St. Merryn

St. Eval

St. Mawgan

Trebelsue

BODMIN

Harrowbeer

Roborough

PLYMOUTH

Perranporth

Portreath

HAYLE

REDRUTH

PENZANCE

Culdrose

FALMOUTH

Predannack

11

NSEA

NEWPORT

Kemble
Babdown Farm
Long Newnton
Hullavington

Stormy Down
Llandow
St. Athan
Rhoose

CARDIFF
Cardiff

Filton

Castle
Combe
Colerne
Charmy Down

BRISTOL

Whitchurch
Lulsgate Bottom

CHANNEL

Weston-super-Mare

Keevil
New
Zealand
Farm

MINEHEAD

FROME

Weston Zoyland

Zeals

Charlton
Yeovilton
Horethorne

Merryfield

Yeovil

Culmhead
Church Stanton

Henstridge

Upottery

Dunkeswell

Tarrant Rushton

DORCHESTER

EXETER

Exeter

Warmwell
WEYMOUTH

Haldon

Portland
BILL of PORTLAND

TORQUAY

12

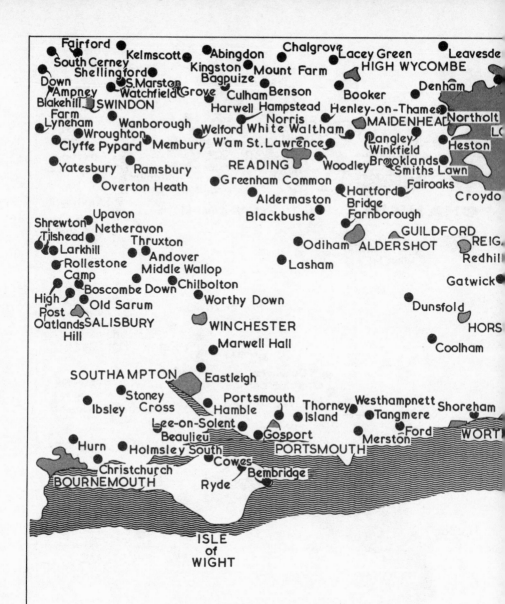

Fairford
Kelmscott
South Cerney
Shellingford
Down
Ampney
Watchfield
Blakehill
Farm
SWINDON
Lyneham
Wanborough
Wroughton
Clyffe Pypard
Membury
Yatesbury
Ramsbury
Overton Heath
Abingdon
Chalgrove
Lacey Green
Leavesde
Kingston
Bagpuize
Mount Farm
HIGH WYCOMBE
S.Marston
Grove
Culham
Benson
Booker
Denham
Harwell
Hampstead
Henley-on-Thames
Norris
MAIDENHEAD
Northolt
Welford
White Waltham
Langley
Heston
W'am St.Lawrence
Winkfield
LO
READING
Woodley
Brooklands
Smiths Lawn
Greenham Common
Hartford
Fairoaks
Bridge
Croydo
Aldermaston
Blackbushe
Farnborough
GUILDFORD
REIG.
Redhill
Gatwick
Dunsfold
HORS
Coolham

Shrewton
Upavon
Tilshead
Netheravon
Larkhill
Thruxton
Rollestone
Andover
Camp
Middle Wallop
Boscombe Down
Chilbolton
High
Old Sarum
Worthy Down
Post
Oatlands
SALISBURY
Hill
Odiham
ALDERSHOT
Lasham
WINCHESTER
Marwell Hall

SOUTHAMPTON
Eastleigh
Stoney
Portsmouth
Thorney
Westhampnett
Shoreham
Ibsley
Cross
Hamble
Island
Tangmere
Lee-on-Solent
Ford
Beaulieu
Gosport
Merston
WORTI
Hurn
Holmsley South
PORTSMOUTH
Christchurch
Cowes
Bembridge
BOURNEMOUTH
Ryde

ISLE
of
WIGHT

ENGLISH

13

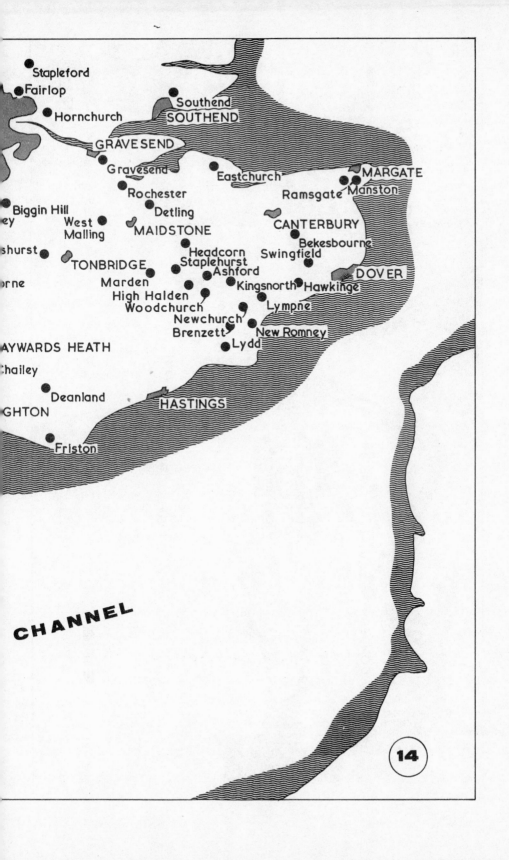

Stapleford
Fairlop
Hornchurch
Biggin Hill
ey
West
Malling
shurst
TONBRIDGE
Marden
orne
High Halden
Woodchurch
Newchurch
AYWARDS HEATH
Chailey
Deanland
GHTON
Friston

Southend
SOUTHEND
GRAVESEND
Gravesend
Rochester
Detling
MAIDSTONE
Headcorn
Staplehurst
Ashford
Kingsnorth
Lympne
Brenzett
Lydd

Eastchurch
CANTERBURY
Bekesbourne
Swingfield
Hawkinge
New Romney

MARGATE
Ramsgate Manston
DOVER

HASTINGS

CHANNEL

14

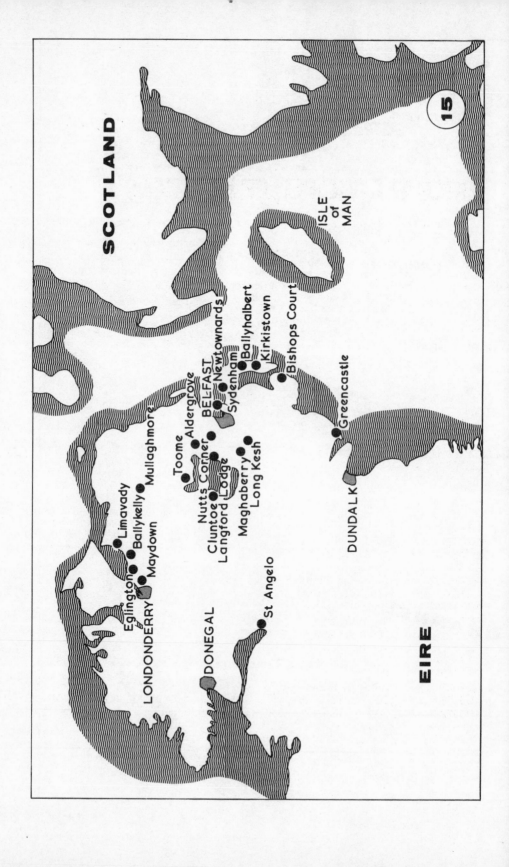

Appendix C

AIRCRAFT PROPELLER NUMBERS

Drawing Ref	Engine	Aircraft type
A5	200 hp Hispano	Vickers Vimy
A21	90 hp Curtiss	Curtiss JN4
A26	Clerget/Le Rhône	Vickers ES2
A50 & 54	300 hp Fiat/R-R Eagle	Vickers Vimy and Vernon
A57	100 hp Monosoupape	Sopwith Pup
AB530	Rolls-Royce Eagle I and II	Handley Page 0/400
AB555	Various rotaries	Avro 504A-K
AB555B	110/130 hp Clerget	Hamble Baby
AB572	240 hp Renault	Short 184
AB586	Sunbeam Cossack	F3 prototype
AB623	200 hp Hispano	Mann Egerton N1A
AB644	Various rotaries	Camel, Nieuport, Avro 504
AB655	Rolls-Royce Eagle V	Porte Baby
AB662	Rolls-Royce Eagle	Curtiss H2
AB662	Wolseley Viper	SE5A, Spad S7
AB662c	200 hp Hispano (ungeared)	SE5A, Dolphin
AB664	Rolls-Royce Eagle VI-VII	HP 0/400, Campania
AB665	Rolls-Royce Eagle VIII	F-Boats, H12, Cork
AB669	Rolls-Royce Eagle VI-VII	Porte Baby, Wight SP
AB682	160 hp Renault	C-Star airships
AB684	150 hp Hispano	Curtiss H4, PV3 and 5
AB685	275 hp Rolls-Royce	DH4
AB693-4	Rolls-Royce Eagle VI-VIII (RH/LH)	Handley Page 0/400
AB703	Siddeley Puma	DH4, DH9
AB705	150 hp Mono Gnome	Sopwith Camel
AB706-7	Sunbeam Maori (LH/RH)	Short 184, Wight, Campania
AB716	Sunbeam Maori	Short N2B and 184
AB723	150 hp Hispano	Spad S7
AB747B	Rolls-Royce Falcon	Avro 529
AB753/757	200 hp Hispano	AD flying boat
AB755/61/65	180 hp Hispano	Spad S7
AB759	150 hp Hispano	Spad S7
AB765/767	180 hp Hispano	SE5A (British/French boss)
AB2442/6	RAF3A	DH4, DH9
AB2627	Siddeley Puma	DH9
AB6238	200 hp Hispano	BE12b, Mann Egerton N1a
AB6622-3	200 hp Hispano and Viper	Cuckoo and AD boat
AB6625/9	Viper and Arab	Bristol Fighter
AB6932-4	Sunbeam Maori	Handley Page 0/400
AB6939/48	Rolls-Royce Eagle VIII (RH/LH)	Handley Page 0/400
AB7031	Siddeley Puma	DH4, DH9, Bristol Fighter
AB7033	230 hp BHP	DH4, DH9
AB7037	Galloway Atlantic	DH4
AB7062/4	Sunbeam Maori	Short 184

Drawing Ref	Engine	Aircraft type
AB7073-5	Sunbeam Maori	Short 184
AB7151-5	Puma and BHP	DH4, DH9
AB7202	200 hp Hispano	Sage 4c
AB7213	190 hp Renault	DH4
AB7282	200 hp Hispano	HP R/200, PV5A
AB7342	Rolls-Royce Eagle VIII	Phoenix P5 Cork
AB7402	200 hp Hispano	Beardmore WBIV
AB7533	Wolseley Viper	AD flying boat
AB7673	Viper and Hispano	SE5A, Dolphin III
AB7790-1	Rolls-Royce Eagle VIII (LH/RH)	Handley Page 0/400
AB7800	Various in-line	HP 0/400, FE pushers
AB7821	260 hp Fiat 12*bis*	Handley Page 0/400
AB7840	220 hp Renault (aft)	Coastal airships
AB7865	260 hp Fiat	DH4, DH9
AB7901/31	Siddeley Puma (HC)	DH9, Bristol Fighter
AB7935	Siddeley Puma	Bristol Fighter, DH9
AB7961	BR2	Austin AFT3, BP P3
AB7981/5/9	200 hp BHP	DH9
AB8080	200 hp Hispano	SE5A, Dolphin
AB8162	Sunbeam Arab	Sage seaplane
AB8210	Sunbeam Arab	Bristol Fighter, Cuckoo
AB8212	BR2 and Arab	Griffin and Cuckoo
AB8224	Sunbeam Arab	Sopwith Cuckoo
AB8381	250 hp Fiat	Parseval No 5
AB8420-2	Rolls-Royce Eagle VIII(T)	Handley Page V/1500
AB8501-3	Rolls-Royce Eagle VIII(P)	Handley Page V/1500
AB8520	Rolls-Royce Eagle VIII	Blackburn Blackburd
AB8551/3	BR1/150 hp Mono	Sopwith Camel
AB8580	Rolls-Royce Eagle VIII(T)	HP V/1500, Blackburd
AB8600	230 hp BHP	FE2h
AB8651	BR2	Sopwith Snipe
AB8680	Rolls-Royce Eagle VIII(T)	Felixstowe Fury
AB8680/91	Rolls-Royce Eagle VIII(T/P)	Felixstowe Fury
AB8701	Rolls-Royce Eagle VIII	Felixstowe Fury
AB8781	Liberty 12	DH9A
AB8831	300 hp Hispano	Bristol Fighter
AB8900	Sunbeam Manitou	Short 184
AB8910	Rolls-Royce Condor	Caproni
AB8951	ABC Dragonfly	RAF Type 1 fighters
AB8961	Curtiss OX5	DH6
AB8973	ABC Dragonfly	Bourges, Weasel
AB8979	ABC Dragonfly	Nighthawk, Siskin protos
AB9180	Sunbeam Arab	Bristol Fighter
AB9331	ABC Dragonfly	BAT Basilisk
AB22699	Liberty	DH9A, DH10, Braemar
ABX4987	Liberty	Handley Page 0/400
AD500	100 hp Monosoupape	FBA, Sopwith Baby
AD501M	225/240 hp Sunbeam	Short 184
AD502	150 hp Sunbeam	Coastal airship (fore)
AD503	90 hp Curtiss OX	Curtiss JN3
AD503	Rolls-Royce Hawk	SSP airship
AD505	250 hp Fiat	R23 airship
AD521	100 hp Green	SS Twin & SSP airship
AD530	250 hp Rolls-Royce	North Sea airship
AD532/535	90 hp RAF/75 hp Renault	BE2c

Drawing Ref	Engine	Aircraft type
AD538-9	250 hp Fiat	R23 airship (fore/aft)
AD543	90 hp Curtiss	JN3/4, DH6, Shorthorn
AD544	250 hp Rolls-Royce	North Sea airship
AD545	Rolls-Royce Eagle I and II	Curtiss H12 and Porte Baby
AD552	100 hp Anzani	Curtiss H4
AB555B	130 hp Clerget	Nieuport Baby
AD555B	110/130 hp Clerget	Hamble Baby Convert
AD555D	110/130 hp Clerget	Schneider/Baby
AD557	240 hp Sunbeam	Short Bomber
AD557	Rolls-Royce Eagle III and IV	Fairey Campania
AD561	Rolls-Royce Hawk	SSP and SS Zero airships
AD564	Rolls-Royce Hawk	Avro, BE2e, MF S11, Sage
AD565-6	225/160 hp Sunbeam	Short 184/827
AD569	Sunbeam Cossack	Handley Page 0/400
AD571M	75 hp Renault	Maurice Farman Shorthorn
AD573	200 hp Canton Unné	Short 166
AD574	Rolls-Royce Eagle V	Wight SP
AD575	Rolls-Royce Eagle III and IV	Handley Page 0/400
AD575M	Rolls-Royce Eagle V	HP 0/400 and Campania
AD581	150/160 hp Sunbeam	Coastal airship (aft)
AD586	Sunbeam Cossack	Curtiss H12
AD587/597	90 hp Curtiss	Curtiss JN3/BE2c
AD598	200 hp Sunbeam	Curtiss R2
AD601M	Rolls-Royce Eagle III, IV, V	Curtiss H12
AD616	160 hp Curtiss	Curtiss R2
AD619	150 hp Hispano	BE2c/e
AD622	75 hp Renault	SSP airship
AD642-3	Rolls-Royce Eagle V	DH4
AD644	Various rotaries	Sopwith Camel, PV9
AD645/6	150 hp Hispano/Arab	AD boat/Sunbeam bomber
AD655	Rolls-Royce Eagle V	HP 0/400 and Porte Baby
AD659	Rolls-Royce Eagle I and II	Handley Page 0/400
AD659	Rolls-Royce Eagle III and IV	Porte Baby
AD664	BR1	Westland N1b
AD671/686	Rolls-Royce Eagle VI-VII	DH4
AD705	BR1/150 hp Gnome Mono	Sopwith Camel
AD707/718	260/240 hp Sunbeam	Wight SP/Short 184
AM1329	Puma or Atlantic	DH9
AM2451	Rolls-Royce Falcon II-III	Bristol Fighter
AM2610-1	Rolls-Royce Eagle VI-VIII	DH4, DH10
AM2627	Siddeley Puma	DH9 and Rhino
AM2628	230 hp BHP	DH10 (Amiens I)
AM5014	RAF3A	DH4
AM5019/29	Liberty 12	DH9A, DH10
BA6358A	Rolls-Royce Falcon I	Blackburn Kangaroo
Brush 2751	80 hp Renault	Maurice Farman
D741/823	150 hp Hispano	Norman Thompson
D923	120 hp Beardmore	Norman Thompson NT2b
D1062	200 hp Hispano	Norman Thompson NT2b/4A
D1465	Sunbeam Arab	Norman Thompson NT2b
D1467/8	200 hp Hispano	Norman Thompson types
FA4441	Sunbeam Maori	Fairey IIIB
FA4441	Rolls-Royce Eagle VIII	Fairey Campania
FA4475M	Sunbeam Maori	Fairey IIIA/B
FA4476	Sunbeam Maori	Fairey III and IIIA

Drawing Ref	Engine	Aircraft type
FA5004	Rolls-Royce Eagle VIII	Fairey IIIC and Campania
FA6194	Rolls-Royce Eagle VIII	Fairey IIIC
FA6952	Rolls-Royce Eagle VIII	Fairey IIIC
GW512/9	200 hp Hispano	Austin-Ball
IPC67A	70 hp Renault	Maurice Farman
IPC70	100 hp Monosoupape	DH2
IPC72 & 127	140 hp Salmson	Henri Farman
IPC2224	200 hp Hispano	Spad
IPC2303	80 hp Renault	Maurice Farman
IPC2360	80 hp Clerget	Sopwith Pup
IPC2365	70 hp Renault	Maurice Farman
IPC2406	80 hp Renault	DH6
IPC2411	Sunbeam Arab	Supermarine Baby
IPC2414	ABC Wasp II	BAT Bantam
IPC3132/78	250/275 hp Rolls-Royce	DH4
IPC23770	RAF1A/80 hp Renault	DH6
LP690	100 hp Monosoupape	Sopwith Baby
LP710C	Various rotaries	Avro, DH5, Pup, 1½ Strutter
LP790	80 hp Renault	BE2c, DH6
LP920	120 hp Beardmore	Elephant and FK8
LP982A	160 hp Beardmore	FE2b
LP1020A	80 hp Clerget/Le Rhône	Sopwith Pup
LP1708	110 hp Le Rhône/Clerget	DH5
LP2100	110/130 hp Clerget	Sopwith Triplane
LP2340	ABC Gnat	PV7 and 8
LP2390A	160 hp Beardmore	AWFK8 and Elephant
LP2400	160 hp Beardmore	Martinsyde Elephant
LP2850	Clerget, Le Rhône, BR1	Sopwith Camel
LP3020	Lorraine-Dietrich	AW FK8
LP3090	Rolls-Royce Falcon	Martinsyde RG
LP3280	200 hp Hispano	Sopwith B1
LP3290	200 hp Hispano	Martinsyde F2
LP3480	200 hp Hispano	Sopwith Cuckoo
LP3500A	200 hp Hispano	Sopwith Dolphin
LP3510	BR1	Sopwith Camel
LP3510A	200 hp Hispano	Sopwith Dolphin
LP3610	200 hp Hispano	Sopwith Dolphin
LP3640	BR1	Sopwith F1 and 2F1 Camel
LP3740	160 hp Beardmore	AW FK8
LP3770A	Rolls-Royce Falcon III	Martinsyde F3
LP3800	200 hp Hispano	Sopwith Dolphin
LP4000	BR2	Snipe, Griffin
LP4020	Siddeley BHP	Sopwith Rhino
LP4030	200 hp Clerget	Sopwith Hippo
LP4040	BR2	Panther, Osprey, Bobolink, Griffin, Snipe
LP5050-70	200 hp Hispano	Sopwith Dolphin
LP5140A	ABC Dragonfly	Sopwith Dragon, Snapper
LP5150	200 hp Hispano	Sopwith B1
LP5250	BR2	Sopwith Snipe
LP5270A/B	300 hp Hispano	Martinsyde F4
LP5300	BR2	Snipe and Salamander
LP 5390	BR2	Sopwith Buffalo
LP5420	300 hp Hispano	Martinsyde F4
P23	110 hp Clerget	Nieuport

Drawing Ref	Engine	Aircraft type
P43	80 hp Le Rhône	Avro 504, Pup, SB3D
P2359	120 hp Beardmore	Bristol TTA
P2408	80 hp Clerget	Bristol Scout C
P3000	80 hp Gnome	Bristol Scout and Pup
P3001	80 hp Le Rhône	Avro 504, Bristol Scout C
P3010	110 hp Clerget	Bristol Scout C
P3012	100 hp Monosoupape	Bristol Scout, Pup, Bantam
P3017	Various rotaries	Bristol Monoplane
P3019	80 hp Clerget	Bristol Scout
P3020	110 hp Le Rhône/BR1	Bristol Monoplane
P3026	Hispano	Bristol F2A Fighter
P3032-3	Rolls-Royce Falcon I-III	Bristol Fighter
P3040	150 hp Hispano	Bristol MR1
P3041	Sunbeam Arab	Bristol Scout F
P3044-5	Rolls-Royce Falcon II-III	Bristol Fighter
P3045-6	Falcon II and III/200 hp Hispano	Bristol Fighter
P3054	BR1/110 hp Le Rhône	Bristol Monoplane
P3060/5	Siddeley Puma (front/rear)	Bristol Braemar I
P3084	Liberty 12 (rear)	Bristol Braemar II
P3120	RAF4A	Armstrong Whitworth FK8
P5071	300 hp Hispano	Bristol Fighter
S75/S132	150 hp Sunbeam/135 hp Salmson	Short 827/830
S134/170	Eagle I/Cossack	Short Bomber, Short 320
S188/239	Canton Unné/Eagle VIII	Short 830, Short Shirl
SC57618	Liberty 12	DH9A (also SC67167)
T1453	70 hp Renault	BE2c
T3277	80 hp Gnome	SE4A
T5014	120 hp Beardmore	RE7
T5291	RAF1A	DH6
T5572	80 hp Renault	BE2c
T5638	160 hp Beardmore	FE2b
T6296/447	RAF4A	BE12/12A, RE8/RE7
T7448	90 hp RAF1A/B	BE2c/d/e, AW FK3
T7531	90 hp RAF1A/B	BE2c/d/e
T7928	100 hp Mono, 110 hp Le Rhône	DH2, FE8
T28005	160 hp Beardmore	FE2b
T28008	RAF4A	BE12/12A, RE8
T28016	90 hp RAF1A	BE2c/d
T28020/3	250 hp Rolls-Royce	FE2d, RE7
T28051-66	150 and 200 hp Hispanos	SE5/SE5A
T28079	275 hp Rolls-Royce	FE2d
T28086-98	150 and 200 hp Hispanos	SE5/SE5A
T28102/2	200 hp Hispano	NE1/CE1
T28137	200 hp Hispano	SE5/SE5A
T28144	Maori, RAF3A	CE1
T28742B	400 hp Liberty	DH9A
T28756A	Napier Lion	DH9A
X3012	Liberty 12	DH4, DH9, DH9A
X4987	Liberty 12	F5L flying boat
Y31	Various rotaries (100-130 hp)	Avro 504A-K
Y80	Various rotaries (80 hp)	Avro 504 variants
Y120	120 hp Beardmore	Martinsyde Elephant
Y503	Clerget/Le Rhône	Avro 504A-K
Y548	Rolls-Royce Condor III	Avro Aldershot
Y559	Napier Lion II	Avro Bison

Appendix D

AMERICAN PROPELLER TYPES

A2/101	Crane I	A5/119	Vengeance I/IA
A2/102	Beechcraft types	A5/120A	Ventura
A2/103	Pitcairn	A5/122	York/Lancaster
A2/104	Vigilant I/IA	A5/123	Warwick I
A2/105	Reliant I	A5/124	Baltimore I-III
A2/107	Beechcraft	A5/125	Liberator I/II
A3/101	Goose I/IA	A5/126	Mosquito
A3/102	Yale I	A5/127	Liberator III/VII
A3/103	Lockheed 12A	A5/129	Dakota I-II
A3/104	Beechcraft types	A5/130	Mitchell I-III
A3/106	Kingfisher	A5/133	Boeing Clipper
A3/107	Seamew I/II	A5/134	Fortress IIA/III
A3/108	Kingfisher	A5/135	Vengeance I-IV
A3/109	Oxford V	A5/136	Thunderbolt
A3/110	Expeditor/Traveller	A5/137	Avenger I-III
A4/101	Chesapeake	A5/138	Lancaster III/X
A4/102	Cleveland	A5/141	Hellcat I
A4/103	Harvard I/II/III	A5/142	Hudson VI
A4/104	Nomad	A5/144	Corsair I-IV
A4/105	Master III	A5/145	DC-4
A4/106	Harvard I, II, III	A5/149	Mustang III-IV
A5/101	Stirling II	A5/150	Warwick I/III
A5/107	Wellington IV	A5/151	Liberator BVI
A5/108	Boston I	A5/153	Fortress IIA
A5/108A	Havoc I	A5/154	Liberator BVI
A5/109	Boston/Havoc	A5/155	Monitor
A5/110	Buffalo	A5/156	Dakota III-IV
A5/111	Catalina I and II	A5/158	Sunderland V
A5/112	Fortress I	A5/159	Lancaster I, III, VII
A5/113-4	Hudson I	A5/160	Mosquito B16, NF30
A5/114	Hudson II	A5/163	Mosquito B16, NF30
A5/115	Hudson III	A5/165	Mosquito PR34, B35, NF36/38
A5/116	Hudson IV/IVA		
A5/117	Hudson V	A5/166	Avenger III
A5/118	Wildcat I/III/IV	A5/170	Liberator V, VI, VIII

Appendix E

GERMAN COMPONENT NUMBERS

To assist those tracing parts of German aircraft wreckage found, the Luftwaffe part numbering system is detailed. German equipment was part-numbered to a rigid system and each aircraft component, unless too small or fragile, was marked with its number as an aid to replacement ordering. These numbers were in two separate series – a *Gerat* or apparatus number for items of official equipment or a *Sach* number, meaning item, for equipment of commercial origin. However, the latter examples were usually found in the early Luftwaffe aircraft before the material categorisation system was introduced in the early 1930s by the Luftwaffe.

Additionally the airframe itself, engines, propellers, instruments and certain apparatus embodied in the airframe, as opposed to being built with it, were given a *Werke Nr,* which was simply a works number or serial number giving its sequence in the amount produced.

General reference numbers consisted of two parts, a material category number and a part number from a block of numbers allotted to a particular category, in the form 66-28967, so that both the category number and the range of numbers related to a particular class of material. In theory this was an unnecessary duplication, in practice it made a clerical error more easily identifiable. Certainly it is a help to aviation archaeologists when dealing with partly obliterated numbers through crash damage or erosion. Originally 95 equipment categories were used, but during the war this was raised to 109 and, since we always seem to have the complication of the exception to the rule, there was an isolated 124 category for special signals equipment.

Luftwaffe equipment categories covered a wide range of military material. Category 20, for example, was horse-drawn vehicles and handcarts. For the archaeological purpose of identifying the type of equipment from numbers found on isolated pieces of wreckage, just the numbers for equipment likely to be carried on aircraft are tabled:

Category	Type of equipment	Part number range
1	Small and personal arms, spares and accessories	33000-33999
2	Machine guns and accessories, early designs	45000-49999
	Machine guns and accessories, late designs	200000-224999
6	Aircraft cannon and accessories	Various ranges
7	Gun mountings on aircraft	Various ranges
8	Airframes and accessories These were a special case, see below	
9	Aero engines and propellers with spares etc	18000-18999

Category	Type of equipment	Part number range
10	Parachutes, safety, rescue and oxygen system items	29600-30699
11	Sea rescue equipment, surface and air	36000-36999
13	Ammunition of all calibres	53000-53999
18	Bomb release gear (initial allocation)	50000-50999
	Bomb release gear (later allocation)	72000-72999
19	Hydraulic, pneumatic and heating systems	21000-21999
		32000-32999
24	Wireless telegraphy and radio telephony apparatus	26000-28999
26	Electrical fittings and standardised switches	Various ranges
35	Photographic equipment (initial allocation)	38000-42999
	Photographic equipment (later allocation)	75500-75999
41	Aircrew clothing and attachments	Various ranges
52	Aircraft instruments (initial allocation)	20000-20999
	Aircraft instruments (later allocation)	22000-22999
75	Navigational equipment other than wireless	23000-23999

To aviation archaeologists, Category 8, concerned with airframes, is of prime importance. For items common to all aircraft, the equivalent of British AGS parts (see page 37), the following part number ranges were allotted: 8-19000 to 8-19999, 8-37000 to 8-37999 and 8-75000 to 8-75499. These numbers and those in the tabled categories were allotted progressively, within the ranges allocated, and had no other significance than relating to a particular part from which the class of equipment could be readily identified. It was different with parts integral to the building of the airframe, where parts were actually numbered according to their position in the aircraft, and the numbers were broken down into several parts.

A typical Messerschmitt Bf109 airframe part number is: 8-109E-501-0302. From the initial figure 8 we know that this relates to part of an airframe, as the category number is always given first. The 109E gives the aircraft type and sub-type. When the equipment system was planned, it was at the time when the designation system of type numbers, (for example, 108, 109 and 110 to Messerschmitt and 111 Heinkel) was introduced. So the second number related to the aircraft type. The sub-type may not always be given, since most changes of sub-type related to engine changes and may have had little or no effect on the airframe. Thus 109E parts could relate to that or later sub-types.

The first number after the type related to the construction area in nine separate groupings as follows: 1 fuselage, 2 undercarriage, 3 ailerons, elevators, tabs and flaps, 4 flying controls, 5 mainplanes, 6 engine mounting, 7 engine installation, 8 fuel tanks and 9 equipment.

As in the example above, the number is 5 for the mainplanes and the adjoining 01 relates to a particular part of the mainplane in an 01, 02, 03 series for port, centre-section and starboard respectively, with other numbers for wingtips (if fitted separately), or other attachments.

The final number related to a component within the main assembly, such as a wing rib, represented by 03 for the third rib, and the adjoining 02 is the number of one of the separate parts that made up the rib.

A similar breakdown was introduced for engine parts with 9 the category number hyphened to the engine type, for example, 9-601 for a DB601 engine, and numbers from 1-9 represented the cylinder block and various systems. The two letters following related to the main assemblies within that system. The last block of numbers related to a further breakdown to individual parts.

In this survey only the system can be given, for the cataloguing of each part would run to tens of thousands of entries covering several volumes.

Complicated as the systems may appear, it was a logical and embracing method, unlike British aircraft part referencing, which had various different systems used by individual manufacturers, plus the RAF's own store vocabulary. As the war progressed and economies in time and effort became necessary, parts that were peculiar to one type could, with little modification, be made suitable for other types. Such parts were numbered in the general Category 8 series, with the master provision registers annotated to give the other parts which could be substituted.

The thorough documentation associated with efficient accounting procedures, before the age of computers, was a major contribution to the German success in maintaining output, in spite of the dispersal of the aircraft industry due to continued Allied raids on the main centres of German aircraft production.

Appendix F

PRO AIR RECORDS

Class	Subject and range
AIR 1	Mainly World War I records extending to 2, 434 document boxes
AIR 2	Air Ministry registered files running into five figures
AIR 3	Airship log books, a total of 64
AIR 4	Aircrew flying log books. The thousands of unclaimed log books belonging to wartime casualties were destroyed at the Ministry of Defence and only some 200 were selected for preservation.
AIR 5	Some 1,500 files and folders of historical air interest
AIR 6	Records of meetings of the Air Board and Air Council
AIR 7	Special personal papers, particularly of senior officers
AIR 8	Records from Chief of the Air Staff's department
AIR 9	Records from the Directorate of Plans, Air Ministry
AIR 10	APs (Air Publications) including SDs (Secret Documents) and CDs (Confidential Documents) which in some cases were downgraded to APs
AIR 11	Files and documents from Cardington on airships. Some 250 items.
AIR 12	Airship and airship engine drawings, ex-RAF Cardington
AIR 13-17	HQ Balloon, Bomber, Coastal, Fighter and Maintenance Command records respectively. Note that these are Headquarters files and folders, not general files of the Commands
AIR 18	Judge Advocate General's papers, eg, courts martial proceedings.
AIR 19	Private office papers
AIR 20	Miscellaneous air records
AIR 21	Judge Advocate General's office, courts martial registers
AIR 22	Periodical returns, summaries and bulletins
AIR 23	Overseas commands
AIR 24-29	Operational record books of, respectively, commands, groups, wings, squadrons, stations, units.
AIR 30	Submission of citations
AIR 31	Whitley Council Minutes concerning conditions of the Civil Service
AIR 32	Flying and Technical Training Command records
AIR 33	Inspector-General's reports
AIR 34	Interpretation reports
AIR 35	Air Component, British Expeditionary Force 1939-40

Class	Subject and range
AIR 36	North-West Expeditionary Force, RAF component
AIR 37	Allied Expeditionary Air Forces and 2nd Tactical Air Force
AIR 38	Transport and Ferry Command records
AIR 39	Army Co-operation Command

The subject and range given is the author's comment on the material, not necessarily the official heading for the range of material.

To give examples of typical documents which could be selected from the catalogued items under the headings above:

AIR 1/625	List of naval aircraft built and building 1916
AIR 1/1056	Scout school January-March 1918 (St Omer)
AIR 1/1190	Martlesham Heath reports
AIR 2/4929	Supplies to Russia 1942-45
AIR 2/6953	Ejection seat type requirements 1944-49
AIR 2/8663	Production of Albemarles 1941-45
AIR 19/498	Delays in Brewster and Vultee aircraft deliveries 1940
AIR 19/550	Mail deliveries by RAF aircraft 1918

The Public Record Office is probably the only place where such records can be perused, for in many cases the copy held is exclusive, unlike published records, of which many copies are distributed.

Appendix G

AIR REPORTS AND RECORDS

Field Service publications

On its formation in April 1918, the RAF issued a series of handbooks to match the existing handbooks of the Royal Navy and Army on general administrative matters and the operation of equipment. Many of these are of great historical interest and representative examples are tabled. The series started at No 1, titled *Instructions for pay duties for units of the RAF.* Of great interest to the Service in general, this and many others are only of marginal interest now. Only those of general historical interest as aeronautica are tabled here, to show the type of information which they contain.

FS number	Subject of representative FS publication
21	Types of British aeroplanes (each type with three-view photos)
28	Standard wireless station RAF
31	Instructional notes on Vickers gun
34	Instructions to airmen in the event of capture
40	War Establishment (France)
64	Installation, maintenance and use of intercommunication telephones in Handley Page aeroplanes and flying boats
71	Handbook of German military and naval aviation (war) 1918
78	War Establishment, Royal Air Force Canada
89	Identification marks on all aircraft (Allied and Enemy)
110	Particulars of W/T apparatus in use in the Royal Air Force
114	Handbook on the Lewis machine gun
116	Handbook on the Camera gun
131	Royal Air Force Peace Establishment
136	Short history of the Royal Air Force (for cadet college use)

Air Publications

The Field Service handbooks were followed in 1920 by a series that continues to this day, the Air Publications (APs), which are dealt with on page 60. To give a better idea of the subjects in the series, a selection of APs holding matter of interest to air enthusiasts is tabled:

AP	Subject of selected Air Publication
125	Short history of the RAF (originally produced as a history of the war in the air 1914-18, this AP was updated in subsequent editions to 1936)

AP	Subject of selected Air Publication
356	Bomb sighting, with a short account of apparatus in use in 1918
388	Descriptive handbook on general instruments and oxygen equipment
392	Descriptive handbook on the Fairey Seaplane Types IIIB and IIIC
627	Rigging notes on Vickers Vimy (Rolls-Royce Eagle VIII engines). This is one of many such volumes for rigging biplanes. Although general arrangement drawings are included they are not necessarily to scale.
653	Schedule of spare parts for the BR2 engines. (Some 200 APs are devoted to spare part numbers for various aircraft and engines.)
790	Recommendations regarding the design of large boat seaplanes
822	Adaptation and translation into French of a glossary of aeronautical terms
825	Notes on the flying of twin-engined aeroplanes (January 1921)
835	Memorandum on the design of tail skids for Service aircraft
843	State of the development of the Airship Service January 1 1917 (ex-CB419)
847	German rigid airships, February 1917 (ex-CB1265)
849	French seaplane bases and anchorages in the English Channel with RNAS facilities, October 1917 (ex-CB1353)
866	The Bristol Fighter MkIV (handbook)
883	Gunnery and armament training
908	Particulars of armament in use in aircraft
950	Handbook on petrol system for the Vickers Vernon
965	Sound signalling from aircraft (ex-CD11)
966	Report on all-metal Staaken monoplane (ex-CD17)
970	Design requirements for aircraft
1076	Rolls-Royce armoured car
1081	The RAF Pocket Book (A general survey of RAF law, equipment, operational procedures, facts and figures, first issued in 1924 and revised 1928, 1932 and 1939)
1098	RAF Flying Training Part III Seaplane Flying
1120-1	Translated abstracts of *Technische Berichte*
1282	Safety equipment manual (Originally a parachute manual, later C volume dealt with dinghies and associated equipment and D volume with airborne air-sea rescue equipment).
1208	Airworthyness handbook for civil aircraft (issued 1932 and 1937)
1354	Air photography – origins and training
1418	Armoured car manual
1480	Silhouettes of RAF Aircraft 1933 (as originally issued. This was expanded into a number of volumes for the aircraft of various countries. Most interesting of all was 1480X which was on experimental aircraft and which had a limited distribution)
1538	Propellers, all types, general information (with various volumes for specific airscrew types)
1550	Report on operations with the occupation of Penjwin, April-May 1927
1608	Report on operations carried out from Aden against Qutebi Tribe, March-May 1934

AP	Subject of selected Air Publication
1679	P & M (Phelan and Moore) motor cycles
1980	How to avoid flying accidents due to weather
2308	Technical notes for Rolls-Royce engines
2576	Glenn Martin gun turrets
2611	British paratroop equipment for C-47 and C-53

APs up to the 4000+ series issued up to 1953 have been released for public perusal.

Summaries and reviews

Before the war, the Air Ministry issued a monthly duplicated Intelligence Summary with information on RAF, Commonwealth and foreign air forces at low security level. This was replaced by a printed Air Ministry weekly Intelligence Summary, of which over 300 issues were promulgated throughout the war. Classified as secret, the numbers of each issue produced rose to over 3,000 by mid-1945.

While this was produced centrally by the Air Minstry, commands produced their own intelligence summaries, and even down to group level there were some monthly summaries printed with illustrations. No 222 Group in the closing stages of the war, at its Indian Ocean bases, even had a printed, illustrated, weekly summary of operations with a three colour cover.

Apart from the Intelligence Summaries, there were Command Reviews. Bomber Command from 1942 issued a large format *Quarterly Review* with large, well-produced photographs. The twelfth and final issue in 1945 gave a detailed summary of the Command's effort over the years 1939-45. Coastal Command issued a summary in similar format each month from the beginning of 1942. Few copies have survived of Command Reviews, although the print figure for each was 750 and upward. Possibly this was due to each copy carrying the marking 'SECRET' and the warning: *'All persons are hereby warned that the unauthorised retention or destruction of this document is an offence against the Official Secrets Acts, 1911-1920'.*

Presumably many such documents were handed in when units disbanded and have been destroyed officially, since for historical purposes only one copy is needed for PRO holding, otherwise storage costs would rise. However, 30 years after the event, all the information in these reviews is now open and copies have surfaced in collectors' hands in recent years. For readers wishing to peruse such documents, it is advised that individual aircraft identities rarely appear, references being made to aircraft according to the squadron and its individual letter.

On the other hand, in intelligence summaries, when detailing enemy aircraft of the period, ie, German, Italian and Japanese, details of works numbers, code letters and camouflage pattern and colours are often given in the reports. Unfortunately, not all intelligence summaries have been made available, not because there are any state secrets to preserve but in the interest of individuals quoted in interrogation reports.

Reports & Memoranda and current papers

The Aeronautical Research Council issues reports; which may be purchased through Her Majesty's Stationery Office (HMSO); from official British aeronautical research and experimental establishments. Most are scientific studies, but a number over the years are of interest to enthusiasts. A brief selection is tabled merely to give an idea of the scope of these R & Ms, as they are known for short.

Number	Title of R & M
498	Protection of aeroplane fabric, September 1915
537	A flight in Rigid Airship R26, May 1918
691	Wasp-engined Avro 'Fireproof' installation, December 1920
694	Sounds of aeroplanes, October 1920
704	Comparative performance of various airscrews of SE5A with Wolseley Viper engine, November 1920
751	Stability of airships, June 1921
778	An electric motor of small diameter for use inside aeroplane models
825	The singing of circular and streamline wires, March 1921
834	The Handley Page Slotted Wing, March 1922
1236	Control of the Fokker FVII-3m aeroplane, March 1927
1422	Experiments on the Hawker Hornbill biplane, August 1932
1576	Spinning of Pterodactyl MkIV
1719	Full scale tests of Hendy Heck with appendix giving pilot's notes, January 1936
1966	Stalling tests on a Blenheim. December 1939
2324	Design of parachutes for large bombs, November 1941
2431	General handling tests of Sikorsky R-4B helicopters (Hoverfly I), October 1946
2507	Aileron tests on a Spitfire, April 1941
2546	Flight tests on Hurricane II Z3687 fitted with special wings of low drag design

From this selective tabling, showing the wide scope of the series, it will be seen that R & M numbering is not in chronological sequence of the date of the report. This is because many of the reports were classified 'secret' or 'confidential' and the R & M publication release was given in later years, whereas a purely academic study might be released immediately.

Some technical libraries hold R & Ms, bound under the title *Annual Technical Reports* up to 1960 when this binding was discontinued. Copies include most of the early series, but as binding lapsed during the war years 1939-45, R & Ms for these years are included, in the main, in so-called Special Volumes, issued after the war.

A similar series, called Current Papers (CPs for short) starting in 1944, also covered design, wind tunnel investigation and tubulence, eg, CP574 was *Turbulence encountered by Ambassador aircraft over Europe, December 1960*. This series ended in 1979 and relevant material has now reverted to the R & M series.

Some of the more recent R & Ms and CPs are available from HMSO shops as detailed below, with prices varying from a few pence to a few pounds depending largely on the size of the report. Lists of these publications can be obtained from HMSO shops quoting Sectional List 8 which was revised in 1980. Many of the earlier R & Ms are now out of print and are not included in current lists. However, if you have access to a technical library holding the annual reports to check on the reference number, then by quoting an R & M number to HMSO an estimate can be obtained of the photostat copying charge.

Published official histories

A complete run-down of the official histories published can be obtained by getting Sectional List 60 from HMSO, supplied free to prospective customers. This is titled *Histories of the First and Second World Wars and Peacetime Series.* Unfortunately key histories like *Defence of the United Kingdom* by Basil Collier are now out of print, as are most of those of the First World War. The HMSO shops at which lists can be obtained are: 80 Chichester Street, Belfast BT1 4JY; 258 Broad Street, Birmingham B1 2HE; Southey House, Wine Street, Bristol BS1 2BQ; 41 The Hayes, Cardiff CF1 1JW; 13a Castle Street, Edinburgh EH2 3AR; 49 High Holborn, London WC1V 6HB (callers only); PO Box 569, London SE1 9NH (Trade and London area mail order); Brazenose Street, Manchester M60 8AS.

Miscellaneous official publications

The RAF List of Officers and the Retired List can be bought from HMSO. Those of the past, issued monthly in the mid-1920s, even listed officers by squadrons and units and gave the squadron aircraft type and number of flights, together with the station location. The November 1925 issue was composed of some 250 pages of small type. Such documents were clearly marked at the top 'FOR OFFICIAL USE' and at the bottom that they were available from HMSO or through any bookseller, price one shilling and sixpence net (7½p)!

For those interested in civil aviation, HMSO stocks maps and documents of ICAO (International Civil Aviation Organisation).

Commonwealth Air Forces documents

From enthusiasts' publications in Australia and Canada, it is evident that much use is being made of the archives of some Commonwealth countries.

The Royal Australian Air Force issued a weekly Command Intelligence Summary for its operations in the Pacific area. Apart from its articles, its continuing daily review of enemy air activity, and its résumé of RAAF Command operations, it was an excellent guide to activities day by day. Every squadrons' sorties were tabled with numbers and types of aircraft involved, type of operation, target or area of operations and bombs and ammunition expended. The Command also issued situation reports daily and regular escape and evasion reports. A numbered series of intelligence memoranda was also issued, eg, No 43 was *Japanese Army Air Service Airplane Tail Emblems.* At least 25 copies of all such reports were sent to the UK for the RAF. What happened to these it is to be wondered, for since they were RAAF documents it is doubtful if a case could be made for their preservation in British archives.

The Royal Canadian Air Force issued a Monthly Review of RCAF operations in North America starting in mid-1943, giving the flying effort statistics separately for Eastern and Western Air Commands. Inevitably this touched on the Battle of the Atlantic, but in this respect the RCN and RCAF issued a joint, glossy, 32-36 page, well illustrated Monthly Operational Review.

American wartime printed air information publications

The US Army and US Navy each promulgated around a dozen periodic publications on air combat matters during World War 2, as tabled.

Army Air Force

Air Forces General Information Bulletin
Army Air Force Command Information Intelligence Series
Military Intelligence Division Air Information Bulletin
Military Intelligence Service Information Bulletin
Military Intelligence Service Intelligence Bulletin
Photo Intelligence Report (Assistant Chief of Air Staff Intelligence issue)
Tactical and Technical Trends (Military Intelligence Division, War Department)
Information Intelligence Summary (Assistant Chief of Air Staff issue)

Additionally, and at lower level, US Air Forces issued their own summaries. Perhaps the most in demand as collector's items are the Intelligence Summaries of the United States Strategic Air Forces in Europe (the 8th & 15th Air Forces). Starting in late 1943, there were weekly issues until the end of the war, covering operations, enemy tactics, target information, raid assessments, articles on German equipment and a weekly bombing summary. Over 1,000 copies of each summary were printed and copies were actually placed on sale in Britain after the war, although officially the documents were still secret.

United States Navy

Air Operations Memorandum, Bureau of Aeronautics
Atlantic Fleet Air Intelligence and Intelligence Summaries
Bureau of Aeronautics Air Information Report
Bureau of Aeronautics Technical Aviation Intelligence Briefs and Reports
Bureau of Aeronautics News Letter
Bureau of Aeronautics Information Summary
Bureau of Aeronautics Confidential Bulletin

Each month, Naval Air Intelligence issued a Subject Index to Air Combat Intelligence Material, some months it ran to nearly 100 pages of small type subject entries. Just one of the thousands of entries in the July 1944 index is *Performance Trials — Zero vs P-51,P-38F,P-39D-1, P-40F Info'l Intel, Sum. No 1, January 28, 1943.*

It is impossible to survey all the documents available in America and those held in Britain relating to American operations. Perhaps the most significant of World War 2 records is the United States Strategic Bombing Survey. The survey originated from a directive by President Roosevelt to conduct an impartial and expert study of USAAF attacks on Germany, and President Truman instituted a similar survey for the bombing of Japan. The reports ran into hundreds of volumes and with the British Intelligence Objectives Sub-Committee most were printed in quantity by Her Majesty's Stationery Office.

INDEX TO APPENDIX B

Below are listed World War 2 airfields with their corresponding map numbers

Holme, 5
Holmsley South, 13
Honeybourne, 9
Honiley, 9
Honington, 10
Hooton Park, 8
Horethorn, 12
Horham, 10
Hornchurch, 14
Horne, 14
Horsham St Faith, 10
Hucknall, 9
Hullavington, 12
Hunsdon, 9-10
Hurn, 13
Husbands Bosworth, 9
Hutton Cranswick, 5

Ibsley, 13
Ingham, 9
Inskip, 4
Ipswich, 10

Jurby, 3

Keevil, 12
Kelmscott, 13
Kelstern, 10
Kemble, 12
Kenley, 13-14
Kiddington, 9
Kidlington, 9
Kimbolton, 9
King's Cliffe, 9
Kingsnorth, 14
Kingston Bagpuize, 13
Kinloss, 1
Kinnell, 2
Kirkbride, 4
Kirkistown, 15
Kirknewton, 2
Kirkpatrick, 4
Kirmington, 5
Kirton-in-Lindsey, 9
Knettishall, 10

Lacey Green, 13
Lakenheath, 10
Langar, 9
Langford Lodge, 15
Langham, 10
Langley, 13
Larkhill, 13
Lasham, 13
Lavenham, 10
Leamington, 9

Leavesden, 13
Leconfield, 5
Leeming, 5
Lee-on-Solent, 13
Leicester East, 9
Leiston, 10
Leuchars, 2
Lichfield, 9
Limavady, 15
Lindholme, 5
Linton-on-Ouse, 5
Lissett, 5
Little Horwood, 9
Little Rissington, 9
Little Snoring, 10
Little Staughton, 9
Little Sutton, 8
Little Walden, 10
Llanbedr, 7
Llandow, 12
Llandwrog, 7
Long Kesh, 15
Long Marston, 9
Long Newton, 12
Longtown, 4
Lossiemouth, 1
Loughborough, 9
Ludford Magna, 9-10
Ludham, 10
Lulsgate Bottom, 12
Luton, 9
Lydd, 14
Lympne, 14
Lyneham, 13

Machrihanish, 2
Macmerry, 2
Madley, 8
Maghaberry, 15
Manby, 10
Manobier, 11
Manston, 14
Marden, 14
Marham, 10
Market Harborough, 9
Marston Moor, 5
Martlesham Heath, 10
Marwell Hall, 13
Matching, 10
Matlask, 10
Maydown, 15
Meir, 8
Melbourne, 5
Melton Mowbray, 9
Membury, 13
Mendlesham, 10

Mepal, 10
Merryfield, 12
Merston, 13
Metfield, 10
Metheringham, 9
Methwold, 10
Middleton St George, 5
Middle Wallop, 13
Mildenhall, 10
Milfield, 2
Millom, 4
Milltown, 1
Molesworth
  Chelveston, 9
Mona, 7
Montford Bridge, 8
Montrose, 2
Moreton in the Marsh, 9
Moreton Valence, 8
Morpeth, 5
Mount Farm, 13
Mountford, 9
Mullaghmore, 15

Neasham, 5
Netheravon, 13
Newchurch, 14
Newmarket, 10
New Romney, 14
Newton, 9
Newtownards, 15
New Zealand Farm, 12
North Coates, 6
North Creake, 10
Northolt, 13
North Killingholme, 5-6
North Leach, 9
North Luffenham, 9
North Pickenham, 10
North Weald, 10
North Witham, 9
Nuneaton, 9
Nuthampstead, 10
Nutts Corner, 15

Oakington, 10
Oakley, 9
Oatlands Hill, 13
Odiham, 13
Okehampton, 11
Old Buckenham, 10
Old Sarum, 13
Orfordness, 10
Orston, 9
Ossington, 9
Oulton, 10